The Great Indian COOKBOOK

Vincent Joseph
Mohammed Ahmed Qureshi

Photographs
Neeraj Paul

Grange
BOOKS

Acknowledgements

The Publisher would like to thank the **Holiday Inn Crowne Plaza Hotel New Delhi**, for making available the kitchens of their restaurant, *Baluchi*, for the preparation and photography of the dishes. The cooperation received during the making of this book from the Management, particularly Ms Anjali Chatterjee and Ms Bhavna Mehrotra of the Public Relations Department is gratefully acknowledged.

Published by Grange Books
An Imprint of Grange Books PLC
The Grange
Grange Yard
London SE1 3AG

© **Lustre Press Pvt. Ltd. 1995**

This edition published 1995

ISBN: 1-85627-659-7

Photographs: *Neeraj Paul*
Design: *Roli Books CAD Centre*
Text Coordination: *B N Varma*
Typesetting: *Monika Raj Malik, Fleming George P.*

Printed and bound by
Star Standard Industries Pte. Ltd., Singapore

Contents

Introduction

$\mathcal{I}$ndian cuisine is famous the world over, possibly on par with the French and the Chinese. For sheer taste and variety of flavours, Indian food is unique, a delight for the connoisseur and new converts alike.

There is a variety of regional traditions in cooking. An extensive choice of seasonings is offered—curry leaves with roasted mustard seeds, roasted cumin and coriander seeds, sugar, garlic, green chillies, turmeric, cloves, cinnamon and nutmeg—which brings out unique flavours from the very hot to the very sweet.

Long standing influences from across the boundaries are still alive in the flourishing tradition of Mughlai cooking in north India. Spectacular meat preparations, curries, the rogan josh, kormas, koftas and biryanis, made from cream, ghee, spices and almonds are among the best known dishes. Kebab, made from marinated or minced meat, is yet another legacy, as indeed the practice of cooking in a tandoor, a clay oven, fired from below.

Varying food habits, depending on the availability of staples, also makes for enormous diversity. In the east the preferred cooking medium is mustard oil, whereas in the west it is groundnut oil. Given the abundance of coconut in the south, coconut oil is often used. Only ghee is common throughout the country, sparingly used these days, but a must for rich and festive cooking.

Presentation of the meal is just as important. The food is laid out in platters or bowls at the beginning of the meal and not served course by course. Traditionally it is eaten off a leaf-plate in the country, generally a banana leaf in the east and the south, and off a thali of brass, stainless steel or even silver in affluent homes. Katoris or small bowls arrayed around it, hold individual helpings of a dish.

A typical meal consists of a portion of chicken, meat or fish, a couple of vegetable curries, dal, yoghurt or raitas accompanied by rice and rotis, not to leave out traditional pickles or chutneys. Water is normally drunk with the meal, alcohol not being quite in the tradition. Sweet meats and paan (betel leaf smeared with catechu and filled with cardamom and betelnut) round off the meal.

This book attempts to bring together a set of recipes, which are not only all time favourites but are easily made in a modern kitchen, an oven or an open charcoal grill or a tandoor. The recipes are grouped together both according to methods of cooking, as well as the types of dishes, the curries, the dals, rotis and accompaniments and lastly, the desserts.

Bon appetit!

Geelafi Seekh Kebab 15

Murgh Khusk Parda 10

Murgh Kastoori 18

Murgh Makhani 21

Murgh Musallam 18

Murgh-e-Khas 16

8

Chicken

Tandoori Chicken

Succulent, mildly spiced, grilled chicken, the best known dish in the entire Indian cuisine!

Serves: 4-5   Preparation time: 6 hours   Cooking time: 20 minutes

Ingredients:

Chicken broiler (600 gms each)	2	**For the marinade:**	
Butter for basting	50 gms/¼ cup	Cumin powder (ground jeera)	5 gms/1 tsp
Chaat masala	5 gms/1 tsp	Garam masala	10 gms/2 tsp
Cream	10 ml/2 tsp	Ginger paste	25 gms/5 tsp
Garlic paste	50 gms/3⅓ tbs	Lemon juice	30 ml/2 tbs
Ginger paste	10 gms/2 tsp	Oil	50 ml/3⅓ tbs
Lemon juice	30 ml/2 tbs	Red chilli paste	25 gms/5 tsp
Onion rings/lemon wedges for garnishing		Saffron	0.5 gms
Red chilli paste	25 gms/5 tsp	Salt to taste	
Salt to taste		Yoghurt, hung	200 gms/1 cup

Method:

Step 1. Clean the chicken, remove the skin and make incisions—3 on each breast and thighs and 2 on each drumstick.

2. Mix the salt, red chilli paste, ginger and garlic pastes and lemon juice and rub this paste into the chicken. Keep aside for 30 minutes.

3. Whisk yoghurt in a large bowl, and add all the ingredients for the marinade.

4. Rub the chicken with the marinade and leave for 5-6 hours in the refrigerator.

5. Preheat the oven or tandoor to 175 ºC (350 ºF).

6. Skewer each chicken from head to tail, leaving a 4 cm gap between the birds. Keep a tray underneath to collect the excess drippings.

7. Roast for approximately 15 minutes or until done in the preheated oven or tandoor. Baste with butter and roast for another 3 minutes.

To Serve:

Remove the chicken from the skewer, cut each chicken into four pieces and arrange on a platter. Sprinkle with chaat masala and cream, garnish with raw onion rings and lemon wedges. Having made tandoori chicken, you can now convert it into the more exotic **Murgh Khusk Parda**! Can be served as a starter as part of a large festive meal, or as part of a tandoori platter mixed with other grilled meats, complemented by a raita, a fresh green salad and rotis.

Murgh Khusk Parda

Tandoori chicken bound with a light pastry covering (parda)—a complete meal in itself!

Serves: 4-5   Preparation time: 40 minutes + 6 hours for tandoori chicken   Cooking time: 20 minutes

Ingredients:

For the parda dough:		Milk	100 ml/½ cup
Butter	50 gms/¼ cup	Salt to taste	
Cream	120 ml/⅔ cup	Sugar	10 gms/2 tsp
Egg yolks	2	Vetivier (kewda)	2 drops
Flour	150 gms/¾ cup		

Method:

Step 1. Follow the master recipe for tandoori chicken till the chicken is half cooked—approximately 5 minutes.
2. Sieve the flour with the salt into a mixing bowl.
3. Dissolve the sugar in warm milk, add the kewda and stir.
4. Pour the milk mixture into the flour, knead into a dough and keep aside for 15 minutes.
5. Add melted butter to the dough, knead the dough again and keep aside for 10 minutes.
6. Divide dough into 2 equal portions, make a ball and dust with flour. Leave aside for another 5 minutes.
7. Grease 2 casserole dishes, one for each chicken.
8. Roll out the dough into discs, the size of each casserole dish. Prick the surface of the dough with a fork.
9. Preheat the oven to 150 ℃ (300 ℉).
10. Cut the chicken into four pieces and arrange in the casserole. Sprinkle half the cream on the chicken and cover with the dough (parda). Brush with beaten egg yolk.
11. Repeat this process with the second chicken and dough.
12. Bake for 10-15 minutes, until the pastry (parda) is golden brown.

To Serve:

Cut open the parda and serve the chicken along with a portion of the parda.

Murgh Kandhari

A well known Indian barbecued chicken delicacy

Serves: 4-5   Preparation time: 4-5 hours
Cooking time: 15 minutes

Ingredients:

Chicken broiler (600 gms each)	2	Lemon juice	40 ml/2⅔ tbs
Black cumin (shah jeera)	3 gms/⅔ tsp	Pomegranate	
Black pepper, crushed	6 gms/1⅓ tsp	juice	40 ml/2⅔ tbs
Butter for basting	40 gms/2⅔ tbs	Red chilli	
Double cream	80 ml/7⅓ tbs	powder	12 gms/2½ tsp
Garam masala	10 gms/2 tsp	Saffron	1 gm
Garlic paste	40 gms/2⅔ tbs	Salt to taste	
Ginger paste	40 gms/2⅔ tbs	Yoghurt, hung	300 gms/1½ cups

Method:

Step 1. Skin the chicken and make deep incisions—3 on each side of the breast, 3 on each side of the thigh and 2 on each drumstick.
2. Mix the red chilli powder, lemon juice and pomegranate juice and rub over the chicken evenly.
3. Marinate for 2 hours in the refrigerator.
4. Whisk the yoghurt in a bowl. Add the ginger and garlic pastes,

cumin, cream, salt, saffron, black pepper and garam masala and mix well.

5. Marinate the chicken in this mixture in the refrigerator for at least 2-3 hours.
6. Preheat the oven or tandoor to 175 °C (350 °F).
7. Skewer the chicken from the tail to head, leaving a gap of at least 4 cm between the birds. Bake in the oven or tandoor for 10 minutes.
8. Remove from the oven, hang the skewers and let the excess moisture drip off the chicken.
9. Baste with butter and roast again for 4-5 minutes.

To Serve:

Remove the chicken from the skewer, sprinkle with lemon juice and serve with roti or naan, green salad, and fresh mint chutney.

Chakundri Tangri Kebab

Tandoori chicken with beetroot

Serves: 4-5   Preparation time: 3 hours   Cooking time: 20 minutes

Ingredients:

Chicken drumsticks	15	Garam masala	10 gms/2 tsp
Beetroot, grated very fine		Garlic paste	25 gms/5 tsp
to marinate chicken	150 gms/¾ cup	Ginger paste	25 gms/5 tsp
Black cumin seeds (shah jeera)	5 gms/1 tsp	Lemon juice	30 ml/2 tbs
Butter for basting	20 gms/4 tsp	Salt to taste	
Cream	80 ml/5¹/₃ tbs	Yoghurt	150 gms/¾ cup

Method:

Step 1. Skin the chicken, and make 2 deep incisions on each drumstick.
2. Make a mixture of lemon juice, beetroot and salt and rub evenly over the chicken legs. Keep aside for at least 1 hour.
3. Whisk yoghurt in a bowl, add the remaining ingredients and mix well.
4. Marinate chicken legs in this mixture and keep in a refrigerator for 2-3 hours.
5. Preheat the oven to 175 °C (350 °F).
6. Skewer the chicken drumsticks, leaving a gap of at least 2 cm between each drumstick. Keep a tray underneath to collect the drippings.
7. Roast in hot tandoor or oven or charcoal grill for about 10-15 minutes.
8. Baste continuously with melted butter. (Basting with melted butter is very important during cooking.)

To Serve:

Serve on a bed of shredded cabbage, garnished with lemon wedges and a spring of parsley.

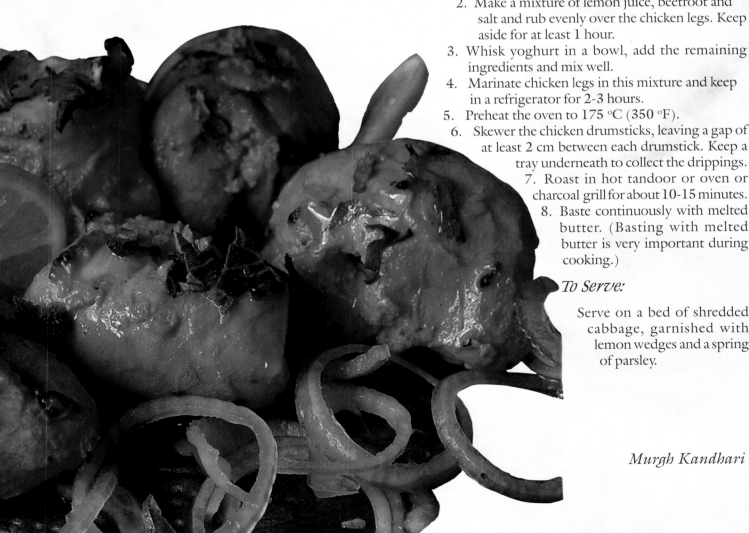

Murgh Kandhari

11

Murgh Afghani Kebab

Chicken kebabs, a speciality of the northwest provinces of India

Serves: 4-5   Preparation time: 4½ hours   Cooking time: 15 minutes

Ingredients:

Chicken broiler (750 gms each)	2	Green chillies, chopped	10 gms/6
Butter for basting	50 gms/3¹/₃ tbs	Mace powder	1.5 gms/¹/₃ tsp
Cheese, grated	100 gms/½ cup	Mace powder, for the vinegar marinade	4 gms/¾ tsp
Cream	60 ml/4 tbs	Malt vinegar	60 ml/¹/₃ cup
Garlic paste	25 gms/5 tsp	Salt to taste	
Ginger paste	25 gms/5 tsp	White pepper powder	10 gms/2 tsp
Green cardamom powder		Yoghurt, hung	400 gms/2 cups
(for the yoghurt marinade)	1.5 gms/¹/₃ tsp		

Method:

Step 1.   Clean, skin and cut each chicken into 12 pieces.

2.   Mix salt, white pepper, mace powder, ginger and garlic pastes with malt vinegar in a large bowl and rub the chicken pieces with the mixture. Marinate for 1 hour.

3.   Mix the yoghurt and grated cheese together and add cream, chopped green chillies, mace and cardamom powder. Mix thoroughly.

4.   Transfer the marinated chicken into yoghurt mixture. Keep aside for 3 hours.

5.   Preheat the oven to 175 °C (350 °F). Skewer the chicken pieces 2 cms apart. Keep a tray underneath to collect the excess drippings. Roast in a moderately hot oven or tandoor for 10-12 minutes.

6.   Remove and hang the skewers to allow the excess moisture to drip off. Baste the chicken with butter and roast for 3 minutes.

To Serve:

Serve the kebabs either on the skewers or separately on a bed of lettuce with lemon wedges. They may be served either as a starter or as a main course accompanied by a raita, green salad, naan or tandoori roti.

Tandoori Motia Tikka

Pungent garlic chicken kebabs

Serves: 4-5   Preparation time: 4 hours   Cooking time: 15 minutes

Ingredients:

Chicken (boneless, cut into cubes)	1 kg
Black cumin (shah jeera)	4 gms/¾ tsp
Black pepper, crushed	6 gms/1¹/₃ tsp
Butter for basting	50 gms/3¹/₃ tbs
Cheese, grated	60 gms/¹/₃ cup
Double cream	60 ml/4 tbs
Garam masala	10 gms/2 tsp
Garlic, sautéed	100 gms/½ cup
Garlic paste	40 gms/2²/₃ tbs
Ginger paste	50 gms/3¹/₃ tbs
Green chilli paste	10 gms/2 tsp
Lemon juice	15 ml/1 tbs
Salt to taste	
Yoghurt, hung	300 gms/1½ cups

Method:

Step 1. Marinate the chicken with half the ginger and garlic pastes, lemon juice and salt for 1 hour.

2. In a bowl mix the yoghurt with all the other ingredients, except the sautéed garlic and butter, and whisk till smooth.

3. Marinate the chicken in this mixture for at least 3 hours.

4. Skewer the chicken pieces 2 cms apart. Preheat the oven to 175 ºC (350 ºF). Press sautéed garlic on the skewered chicken and roast in a tandoor/oven, or grill for 8-10 minutes. The garlic will appear golden in colour on the chicken.

5. Baste with butter and roast for another 3 minutes.

To Serve:

Serve with mint chutney, garnished with sliced cucumber, tomatoes and onions.

Kastoori Kebab

An egg-coated chicken preparation, spiced with cumin and fenugreek and flavoured with cardamom

Serves: 4-5   Preparation time: 1 hour   Cooking time: 15 minutes

Ingredients:

Chicken breasts	12	Gram flour (besan)	10 gms/2 tsp
Black cumin seed (shah jeera)	3 gms/²/₃ tsp	Green cardamom powder	2 gms/½ tsp
Bread crumbs	20 gms/4 tsp	Green coriander, chopped	20 gms/4 tsp
Butter	60 gms/4 tbs	Lemon juice	45 ml/3 tbs
Egg yolks	3	Oil	10 ml/2 tsp
Fenugreek, dried (kasoori methi)	30 gms/2 tbs	Saffron	0.5 gms
Garlic paste	40 gms/2²/₃ tbs	Salt to taste	
Ginger, chopped	20 gms/4 tsp	White pepper powder	5 gms/1 tsp
Ginger paste	40 gms/2²/₃ tbs		

Method:

Step 1. Clean the chicken, skin, debone and cut each breast into two.

2. Mix ginger and garlic pastes, fenugreek, pepper and salt with the lemon juice and rub the chicken breast with the mixture. Keep aside for at least 1 hour.

3. Heat butter and oil in a pan, add gram flour and stir over medium heat until golden brown. Divide this mixture into two parts.

4. To one part add bread crumbs, chopped ginger, fresh coriander and marinated chicken. Mix well so that the chicken is coated with the marination.

5. Preheat oven to 150 ºC (300 ºF).

6. To the second part of the gram flour add cumin, saffron and the egg yolks and whisk batter thoroughly.

7. Skewer 6 chicken pieces together so that they overlap. Leave a gap of 4 cms and then skewer the next lot. Coat each with the gram flour batter as in Step 6.

8. Roast the chicken in the oven or tandoor for 8-10 minutes.

9. Remove and sprinkle with cardamom powder and lemon juice.

To Serve:

Serve with a green salad.

Murgh Afghani Kebab
Tandoori Motia Tikka
Kastoori Kebab

Reshmi Seekh Kebab

Minced chicken kebabs on skewers

Serves: 4-5   Preparation time: 30 minutes   Cooking time: 10 minutes

Ingredients:

Chicken, minced	1 kg	Ginger paste	20 gms/4 tsp
Butter for basting	50 gms/3$^1/_3$ tbs	Green chillies, chopped	15 gms/3 tsp
Cashewnut paste	50 gms/3$^1/_3$ tbs	Green coriander, chopped	15 gms/3 tsp
Cottage cheese (paneer), grated	50 gms/3$^1/_3$ tbs	Oil	60 ml/4 tbs
Cumin powder (jeera)	10 gms/2 tsp	Onions, chopped	50 gms/3$^1/_3$ tbs
Eggs, whisked	2	Salt to taste	
Garam masala	5 gms/1 tsp	White pepper powder	5 gms/1 tsp
Garlic paste	20 gms/4 tsp	Yellow chilli powder (deghi mirch)	5 gms/1 tsp

Method:

Step 1. To the minced chicken, add cumin powder, white pepper, yellow chillies, salt and oil and mix well. Keep aside for 15 minutes.

2. Then add the cashewnut paste, ginger and garlic pastes, onions, green chillies, coriander, garam masala, grated paneer and eggs. Mix well.

3. Divide the mixture into 8 equal portions and make balls. Pass the skewer through the balls of mince. Moisten your hands and spread the balls by pressing each along the length of the skewers until they are 8-10 cms long and about 4 cm apart.

4. Roast in a hot tandoor or oven to 175 ºC (350 ºF) for 8-10 minutes, basting with butter and roasting until golden brown.

To Serve:

Serve as a starter, garnished with onion rings and lemon wedges.

Mughlai Murgh Shikanj

Geelafi Seekh Kebab

An exotic and colourful kebab!

Serves: 4-5   Preparation time: 20 minutes   Cooking time: 8-10 minutes

Ingredients:

Chicken, minced	800 gms	Ginger, chopped	20 gms/4 tsp
Butter for basting	50 gms/3^1/$_3$ tbs	Green chillies, chopped	15 gms/6
Capsicum (green pepper), chopped fine	10 gms/2 tsp	Green coriander, chopped	15 gms/3 tsp
Cashewnut paste	50 gms/3^1/$_3$ tbs	Lemon juice	30 ml/2 tbs
Chaat masala	5 gms/1 tsp	Oil	40 ml/2^2/$_3$ tbs
Cottage cheese (paneer), grated	50 gms/¼ cup	Onions, chopped fine	10 gms/2 tsp
Cumin powder (jeera)	10 gms/2 tsp	Salt to taste	
Eggs, whisked	2	Tomatoes, chopped fine	10 gms/2 tsp
Garam masala	5 gms/1 tsp	White pepper powder	5 gms/1 tsp
Garlic paste	20 gms/4 tsp	Yellow chilli powder (deghi mirch)	5 gms/1 tsp

Method:

Step 1. Add the whisked eggs, cumin powder, yellow chillies, white pepper, salt and oil to the minced chicken, and mix well. Keep aside for 15 minutes.
2. Add to the chicken mince the cashewnut paste, chopped ginger, chillies, garlic paste, green coriander, onions, grated paneer and garam masala, and mix well.
3. Divide into 8 equal portions and make into balls. Skewer the balls of mince. With wet hands spread the balls by pressing each along the length of the skewers to make 10 cm long kebabs, 4 cm apart.
4. Mix capsicum, tomato and gently press over the skewers evenly from top to bottom.
5. Roast in a hot oven to 175 ℃ (350 ℉) for 8-10 minutes, basting melted butter and roast until golden brown.

To Serve:

Sprinkle chaat masala and lemon juice, and serve, garnished with onion rings and lemon wedges.

Mughlai Murgh Shikanj

Egg and cheese-coated chicken legs

Serves: 4-5   Preparation time: 1½ hours   Cooking time: 15 minutes

Ingredients:

Chicken drumsticks, skinned and deboned	5	Ghee (clarified butter)	100 gms/½ cup
Black pepper, crushed	5 gms/1 tsp	Green chilli paste	5 gms/1 tsp
Butter	40 gms/2^2/$_3$ tbs	Lemon juice	3 ml/^{2}/$_3$ tsp
Cornflour	20 gms/4 tsp	Mace powder (javitri)	3 gms/^{2}/$_3$ tsp
Cottage cheese (paneer), grated	50 gms/3^1/$_3$ tbs	Nutmeg powder (jaiphal)	3 gms/^{2}/$_3$ tsp
Cream	40 ml/2^2/$_3$ tbs	Salt to taste	
Eggs	2	Yoghurt, hung	80 gms/5^1/$_3$ tbs
Garam masala	5 gms/1 tsp		

Method:

Step 1. With a steak hammer flatten the deboned chicken drumsticks and arrange them on a platter.
2. Make a paste of the nutmeg, black pepper, garam masala and green chillies. Rub the paste on the chicken pieces. Keep aside for an hour.
3. In a bowl combine all the other ingredients to a fine creamy consistency.
4. Marinate the chicken in this mixture for further half an hour
5. Heat the ghee in a pan over medium heat, and shallow fry the chicken pieces till crisp and golden.

To Serve:

Serve accompanied by lemon wedges, green salad and mint chutney.

Farag-e-Potli

A haggis-like speciality made with the neck of the chicken!

Serves: 4-5   Preparation time: 40 minutes   Cooking time: 40 minutes

Ingredients:

Chicken necks, outer skin only, without the centre neck bone, cleaned thoroughly	5 pieces
or	
Chicken breasts, skinned and flattened with a steak hammer	5 pieces
Chicken, minced	900 gms
Aniseed powder	3 gms/²/₃ tsp
Any soft cheese, grated	25 gms/5 tsp
Black pepper powder	5 gms/1 tsp
Butter to baste	100 gms/½ cup
Cream	20 ml/4 tsp
Egg	1
Garam masala	10 gms/2 tsp
Garlic paste	30 gms/6 tsp
Ginger paste	30 gms/6 tsp
Green chilli paste	8 gms/1²/₃ tsp
Green coriander, chopped	10 gms/2 tsp
Lemon juice	15 ml/1 tbs
Nutmeg (jaiphal), grated	½ nutmeg
Onions, grated	40 gms/2²/₃ tbs
Salt to taste	

Farag-e-Potli

Method:

Step 1. Mix all the ingredients except for the chicken necks or chicken breasts, with the chicken mince, and keep in the refrigerator for 30 minutes.

2. Divide the mixture into 5 portions, and make into balls for stuffing the breast or neck.

3. Stuff each neck right through with a portion of the mixture and tie a thread on both ends of the stuffed necks. Or if using breasts, place each ball in the centre of the chicken breast, wrap, shape like a haggis, and tie with the kitchen thread.

4. Heat the oven to 150 °C (300 °F).

5. Grease the roasting tray, arrange the stuffed necks or stuffed chicken breasts on it and dot with a little butter. Roast for 30-40 minutes, turning constantly and basting with melted butter, until the skins are golden in colour.

To Serve:

Remove the threads, arrange the chicken on a serving platter and serve hot with green salads and mint chutney.

Murgh-e-Khas

Chicken kebabs stuffed with nuts

Serves: 4-5   Preparation time: 45 minutes   Cooking time: 20 minutes

Ingredients:

Chicken legs, whole	4	Green chilli paste	25 gms/5 tsp
Chicken, minced	300 gms	Groundnut oil	15 ml/3 tsp
Almonds	50 gms/3¹/₃ tbs	Lemon juice	30 ml/2 tbs
Cashewnuts	50 gms/3¹/₃ tbs	Lemon wedges and tomato slices for garnishing	
Cream	100 ml/½ cup	Mint chutney	100 gms/½ cup
Garam masala	5 gms/1 tsp	Saffron	1 gm
Garlic paste	25 gms/5 tsp	Salt to taste	
Ginger paste	25 gms/5 tsp		

Method:

Step 1. Debone the entire chicken leg, leaving only the top of the drumstick. Flatten the chicken leg using a steak hammer.
2. Make a marinade with half the quantity of ginger and garlic paste, salt, green chilli paste and lemon juice. Marinate the chicken in this and refrigerate for half an hour.
3. Chop the almonds and cashewnuts and mix with the chicken mince and chutney.
4. Add garam masala and the remaining ginger, garlic, green chilli pastes, salt and lemon juice to the mince mixture and mix well.
5. Stuff the deboned chicken with this mixture, rolling the chicken in such a way that the mince is wrapped in it.
6. Grease a baking tray with the groundnut oil. Place the rolls on the tray and cover with foil. Bake in a medium oven to 100 ºC (200 ºF) until done (approximately 20 minutes).
7. Take the chicken out of the oven and remove the foil. Slice each chicken roll diagonally and arrange on a platter.
8. Pour the saffron mixed with cream over the sliced chicken.

To Serve:

Serve hot, garnished with lemon wedges and tomato slices.

Saag Murgh

Chicken curried in a spicy spinach purée

Serves: 4-5   Preparation time: 10 minutes   Cooking time: 45 minutes

Ingredients:

Chicken, skinned and cut into pieces	1 kg	Oil	60 ml/4 tbs
Bay leaves (tej patta)	2	Onion paste	200 gms/1 cup
Butter	100 gms/½ cup	Red chilli powder	10 gms/2 tsp
Cinnamon sticks	4	Salt to taste	
Fenugreek powder (methi)	3 gms/²/₃ tsp	Spinach (palak), puréed	350 gms/1¾ cups
Garlic paste	40 gms/2²/₃ tbs	Tomatoes, chopped	180 gms/¾ cup
Ginger juliennes	10 gms/2 tsp	Water	40 ml/2²/₃ tbs
Ginger paste	40 gms/2²/₃ tbs	White pepper powder	3 gms/²/₃ tsp
Maize flour (makke ka atta)	3 gms/²/₃ tsp		

Method:

Step 1. Heat the oil in a pan, add the whole spices (cinnamon and bay leaves), and sauté over medium heat until they begin to crackle.
2. Add the ginger, garlic and onion pastes and red chilli powder, and sauté for 30-60 seconds.
3. Add tomatoes and sauté further for 1 minute.
4. Add the spinach purée, stir in maize flour diluted with water and cook over medium heat for 10-15 minutes, stirring occasionally.
5. In another pan heat the butter and sauté the chicken until lightly browned.
6. Transfer the chicken pieces into the spinach sauce. Add salt and white pepper powder, cover and simmer on very low heat (*dum*) for 10-15 minutes or till chicken is cooked.

To Serve:

Serve garnished with ginger juliennes and fenugreek powder.

Saag Murgh

Murgh Kastoori

As with almost every fenugreek delicacy Methi Murgh tastes best with fresh fenugreek

Serves: 4-5   Preparation time: 45 minutes   Cooking time: 30 minutes

Ingredients:

Chicken, boneless	1 kg	Ginger juliennes	10 gms/2 tsp
Bay leaves (tej patta)	2	Green cardamoms	10
Black cardamoms	2	Green chillies, slit,	
Black cumin (shah jeera)	3 gms/^{2}/$_3$ tsp	deseeded and chopped	15 gms/3 tsp
Cinnamon sticks	2	Mace powder (javitri)	5 gms/1 tsp
Cloves	8	Onions, chopped	30 gms/6 tsp
Coriander, chopped	15 gms/3 tsp	Red chilli powder	8 gms/1^2/$_3$ tsp
Coriander powder	8 gms/1^2/$_3$ tsp	Refined oil	150 ml/¾ cup
Fenugreek powder (methi) or	15 gms/3 tsp	Salt to taste	
Fresh fenugreek	200 gms/1 cup	Tomatoes, chopped	180 gms/¾ cup
Garam masala	10 gms/2 tsp	Turmeric powder (haldi)	5 gms/1 tsp
Garlic, chopped	30 gms/6 tsp	Water	240 ml/1¼ cups
Ginger, chopped	50 gms/3^1/$_3$ tbs	Yoghurt	225 gms/1¼ cups

Method:

Step 1.   Cut the chicken into 15 pieces.
2.   Whisk the yoghurt in a large bowl, add salt and marinade the chicken in this mixture for at least 30 minutes.
3.   Heat the oil in a heavy bottomed pan. Add the whole spices (cardamoms, cloves, cinnamon sticks and bay leaves) and sauté over medium heat for a few minutes.
4.   Add the black cumin, onions and sauté until golden brown.
5.   Add the garlic, ginger and green chillies, stir for 2 minutes. Add the turmeric, coriander and red chilli powder.
6.   Add 60 ml (4 tbs) of water and stir for 30 seconds.
7.   Add the tomatoes and cook over medium heat until the oil separates from the mixture.
8.   Add the marinated chicken along with the marinade and 180 ml (¾ cup) of water, bring to a boil, cover and simmer until chicken is almost cooked and the oil separates from the sauce once again.
9.   Adjust the seasoning.
10.   Sprinkle fenugreek powder, mace powder, garam masala, ginger juliennes and green coriander. (If fresh fenugreek is used, chop and cook it with the chicken.) Cover and cook for 5 minutes more.

To Serve

Serve hot, garnished with green coriander leaves and accompanied by rice or rotis.

Murgh Musallam

Whole chicken stuffed with nuts in a rich creamy sauce

Serves: 4-5   Preparation time: 25 minutes   Cooking time: 45 minutes

Ingredients:

Chicken, whole, skinned	900 gms	Onion paste	160 gms/¾ cup
Almond paste	15 gms/3 tsp	Poppy seed paste	15 gms/3 tsp
Almonds, fried	25 gms/5 tsp	Red chilli powder	10 gms/2 tsp
Black pepper powder	6 gms/1^1/$_3$ tsp	Saffron	1 gm
Cinnamon sticks	4	Salt to taste	
Cloves	10	Silver leaves (varq)	1
Coriander powder	10 gms/2 tsp	Vetivier (kewda)	2 drops
Cream	30 ml/2 tbs	Yoghurt	200 gms/1 cup
Fennel seeds (saunf)	10 gms/2 tsp		
Fresh coconut paste	150 gms/¾ cup	**For the stuffing:**	
Gram flour (besan)	100 gms/½ cup	Almonds	100 gms/½ cup
Green cardamoms	8	Chicken, minced	800 gms
Green coriander, chopped	8 gms/1^2/$_3$ tsp	Cognac (optional)	45 ml/3 tbs
Nutmeg (jaiphal)	3 gms/^{2}/$_3$ tsp	Cream	20 ml/4 tsp
Oil	100 ml/½ cup	Ginger paste	5 gms/1 tsp

Green chilli paste	6 gms/1$^{1}/_{3}$ tsp	Raisins	15 gms/3 tsp
Mace (javitri)	3 gms/$^{2}/_{3}$ tsp	Salt to taste	
Pistachios	25 gms/5 tsp		

Method:

Step 1. In a paraat/bowl combine all the ingredients for the stuffing and fill it into the stomach cavity of the dressed chicken.
2. In a pan, heat the oil and fry the stuffed chicken until it is golden brown. Keep aside.
3. In the same pan add the cardamoms, fennel seeds, cinnamon sticks, cloves and onion paste, and sauté for 30-60 seconds. Add red chilli powder, black pepper, salt and coriander powder, and cook over medium heat for 5-10 minutes.
4. Add the poppy seed paste, almond paste, coconut paste and 2 cups of hot water and bring to a slow boil.
5. Place the chicken in the centre of this sauce, cover and allow to cook on a very low heat until the chicken is completely cooked.
6. Remove the chicken and strain the sauce and add saffron, cream, nutmeg and kewda to the sauce.

To Serve:

Place chicken on a serving dish. Pour the sauce over the chicken and garnish with almonds, silver leaves and green coriander leaves.

Kadhai Murgh Afghani

Kadhai cooking originated with this hot chicken delicacy, cooked in tomatoes

Serves: 4-5   Preparation time: 20 minutes   Cooking time: 30 minutes

Ingredients:

Chicken	1 kg	Green chillies, chopped	4
Coriander seeds, roughly ground	6 gms/1$^{1}/_{3}$ tsp	Green coriander, chopped	20 gms/4 tsp
Fenugreek powder (methi)	4 gms/$^{3}/_{4}$ tsp	Oil	90 ml/6 tbs
Garam masala	10 gms/2 tsp	Red chillies, whole	8
Garlic paste	20 gms/4 tsp	Salt to taste	
Ginger, chopped	30 gms/6 tsp	Tomatoes, chopped	1 kg/5 cups

Method:

Step 1. Skin the chicken and cut into 8 pieces.
2. Grind red chillies and coriander seeds with a little water into a paste.
3. Heat the oil in a deep *kadhai*/wok, add garlic paste and sauté over medium heat until it is light brown. Add the red chilli and coriander seeds, and the tomatoes and cook over   medium heat for 5-10 minutes.
4. Add the green chillies, ginger   and one-third of the green coriander, reduce the heat   and simmer for 4-5 minutes.
5. Add the chicken pieces and salt. Reduce the heat, cook for 10-15 minutes with cover lid on. Stir occasionally, until the oil separates from the mixture, the gravy becomes thick and the chicken tender.
6. Sprinkle with the garam masala and fenugreek and stir for 2 minutes.

To Serve

Garnish with ginger and green coriander. Serve with either steamed rice or Indian bread.

Kadhai Murgh Afghani

Murgh Begam-Bahar

Chicken curry garnished with lamb brain

Serves: 4-5   Preparation time: 15 minutes   Cooking time: 30 minutes

Ingredients:

Chicken	1 kg	Hot water	30 ml/2 tbs
Bay leaves (tej patta)	2	Lamb brain (par boiled)	100 gms/½ cup
Butter	20 gms/4 tsp	Oil	80 ml/5⅓ tbs
Cashewnut paste	100 gms/½ cup	Onions, chopped	200 gms/1 cup
Cinnamon sticks (1 cm)	3	Red chilli powder	8 gms/1⅔ tsp
Cloves	8	Salt	15 gms/3 tsp
Cream	80 ml/5⅓ tbs	Turmeric powder (haldi)	6 gms/1⅓ tsp
Fenugreek (methi) powder	2 gms/½ tsp	Yoghurt, whisked	150 gms/¾ cup
Garam masala	15 gms/3 tsp		
Garlic paste	25 gms/5 tsp	**For parboiling the brain:**	
Ginger paste	25 gms/5 tsp	Salt	10 gms/2 tsp
Green cardamoms	8	Turmeric (haldi)	5 gms/1 tsp
Green coriander, chopped	15 gms/3 tsp	Water	½ litre

Method:

Step 1. Clean and skin the chicken and cut into 8 pieces.

2. Heat the oil in a heavy bottomed pan over medium heat. Add the bay leaves, cinnamon sticks, green cardamoms and cloves and sauté over medium heat till they crackle.

3. Add the chopped onions, turmeric powder and red chilli powder and sauté for another 30 seconds.

4. Add the ginger and garlic pastes and cashewnut paste, and sauté for another 30 seconds.

5. Add the chicken pieces, stir and cook for 10-15 minutes on medium heat.

6. Add the salt and yoghurt. Add hot water. Cover and simmer for 10 minutes on low heat. Add the cream, garam masala and fenugreek powder.

7. For parboiling the brain, bring the water to boil along with the salt and turmeric. Add the lamb brain and lower heat. Once the brain rises to the top, remove it from the pan and keep aside.

8. In another pan, heat the butter and sauté the lamb brain for 2-3 minutes. Break it up with the help of spoon.

To Serve:

Transfer the chicken to a serving dish, and garnish with the fried brain and chopped green coriander.

Murgh Begam-Bahar

Murgh Makhani

Chicken, simmered in butter and tomato curry, a favourite of most north Indians

Serves: 4-5   Preparation time: 20 minutes + time to roast the chicken, if tandoori chicken is not available
Cooking time: 25 minutes

Ingredients:

Tandoori chicken * (cut into 8 pieces each)	2	Green cardamoms	10
Bay leaf	1	Green chillies (slit and deseeded)	5
Butter	120 gms/$^2/_3$ cup	Green coriander, chopped	15 gms/3 tsp
Cinnamon sticks	2	Honey	1 tbs
Cream	150 ml/$^3/_4$ cup	Paprika or red chilli powder	5 gms/1 tsp
Garlic paste	50 gms/$3^1/_3$ tbs	Salt to taste	
Ginger juliennes	10 gms/2 tsp	Tomatoes, chopped	900 gms/$4^1/_2$ cups
Ginger paste	50 gms/$3^1/_3$ tbs	Water	200 ml/1 cup

Method:

* For **Tandoori Chicken** recipe please refer to page 9.

Step 1. Melt half the butter in a thick bottom pan, sauté for 30 seconds the cinnamon, cardamoms and bay leaf, stir in the ginger and garlic pastes, and cook till the water evaporates.

2. Add tomatoes and salt and cook till the tomatoes dissolve. Add 2 cups of water and let it simmer for some time.

3. Strain the gravy through a soup strainer into another pan.

4. Melt the remaining butter in a *kadhai*/wok, add the ginger juliennes and green chillies and sauté for a minute. Add the paprika—the colour of the mixture will turn a bright red. Add the strained gravy and bring to a boil.

5. Add the tandoori chicken pieces and simmer for 10 minutes till the chicken gets soft. Stir in the cream and honey.

To Serve:

Serve garnished with green coriander and accompanied by any Indian bread.

Murgh Shahjahani

A chicken recipe from the kitchens of the Mughal emperors

Serves: 4-5   Preparation time: 15 minutes   Cooking time: 45 minutes

Ingredients:

Chicken, skinned and cut into 8 pieces	1 kg	Ginger juliennes	5 gms/1 tsp
Bay leaves (tej patta)	2	Ginger paste	25 gms/5 tsp
Black cardamom powder	3 gms/$^2/_3$ tsp	Green cardamoms	8
Black cumin (shah jeera)	3 gms/$^2/_3$ tsp	Hot water	200 ml/1 cup
Cashewnut paste	100 gms/$^1/_2$ cup	Oil	80 ml/$5^1/_3$ tbs
Cinnamon sticks (1 cm)	3	Onions, chopped	200 gms/1 cup
Cloves	8	Salt to taste	
Coriander, chopped	15 gms/3 tsp	Turmeric powder (haldi)	6 gms/$1^1/_3$ tsp
Cream	40 ml/$2^2/_3$ tbs	Yellow chilli powder	8 gms/$1^2/_3$ tsp
Eggs (soft boiled and quartered)	3	Yoghurt, whisked	150 gms/$^3/_4$ cup
Garlic paste	25 gms/5 tsp		

Method:

Step 1. Heat the oil in a heavy thick bottomed pan over medium heat. Add the bay leaves, cinnamon sticks, green cardamoms, black cumin and cloves, and sauté until the spices begins to crackle.

2. Add onions, turmeric powder and yellow chilli powder, and sauté for 30 seconds.

3. Add ginger, garlic and cashewnut pastes and sauté for 30 seconds more.

4. Add chicken pieces and cook for 10-15 minutes over medium heat.

5. Add whisked yoghurt with 2 cups of hot water and salt. Cover and simmer for 10-15 minutes on a very low heat.

6. Add the cream and cardamom powder and stir.

To Serve:

Serve garnished with the eggs, green coriander and ginger juliennes.

Murgh Badam Pasanda

A chicken steak with almonds cooked in a heavy copper griddle or pan known as lagan

Serves: 4   Preparation time: 1¼ hours   Cooking time: 20 minutes

Ingredients:

Chicken breasts, skinned	8 pieces	Green coriander	20 gms/4 tsp
Almonds, sliced	25 gms/5 tsp	Mace powder (javitri)	2 gms/½ tsp
Black pepper powder	2 gms/½ tsp	Milk	15 ml/1 tbs
Chicken stock	1 ltr/5 cups	Onions, chopped	100 gms/½ cup
Cloves	10	Red chilli powder	5 gms/1 tsp
Flour	10 gms/2 tsp	Saffron (dissolved in 15 ml of milk)	1 gm
Garlic paste	50 gms/3⅓ tbs	Salt to taste	
Ghee (clarified butter)	100 gms/½ cup	Tomatoes	250 gms/1 cup + 3⅓ tbs
Ginger paste	50 gms/3⅓ tbs	Yoghurt, hung	250 gms/1 cup + 3⅓ tbs
Green cardamoms	10		

Method:

Step 1. Brown the almonds in ghee.
2. Clean and flatten the chicken breasts till about 3 cm thick.
3. Rub the ginger paste over the chicken breasts.
4. Whisk the yoghurt in a large bowl and add the garlic and salt, and rub this mixture into the chicken. Keep aside for 1 hour.
5. Preheat the *lagan* (griddle) and pour half the ghee on it. Place the chicken breasts on it and cook, turning over once until half done. Remove from the *lagan* and keep aside.
6. Add the remaining ghee to the *lagan* and sauté green cardamoms and cloves till they crackle. Then add onions and cook till brown. Add tomatoes, red chilli powder, flour, black pepper, cloves and chicken stock. Cook until the gravy becomes rich and thick.
7. Place the chicken in the gravy and cook, turning it over gently for another 10 minutes.
8. Add the mace powder and the saffron dissolved in a little warm milk.

To Serve:

Serve garnished with the fried almonds and green coriander.

Murgh Galouti Kebab

Chicken mince patties—a Rajasthani speciality

Serves: 4-5   Preparation time: 1½ hours   Cooking time: 10 minutes

Ingredients:

Chicken, minced	1 kg	Ginger paste	40 gms/2⅔ tbs
Butter	50 gms/3⅓ tbs	Green cardamom powder	5 gms/1 tsp
Cottage cheese (paneer), grated	50 gms/3⅓ tbs	Red chilli powder	5 gms/1 tsp
Garlic paste	40 gms/2⅔ tbs	Roasted gram flour (besan)	15 gms/1 tbs
Ghee (clarified butter)	100 gms/½ cup	Salt to taste	

Method:

Step 1. Mix all the ingredients with chicken except for ghee and let it stand for at least 45 minutes to 1 hour.
2. Put the minced chicken in the refrigerator for 15 minutes.
3. Divide the mixture into 32 equal portions and make balls.
4. Dip your hand in chilled water and press each ball between the palms to a round disk of 5 cm diameter.
5. Heat ghee on a hot plate or griddle and shallow fry the patties over low heat until both sides are evenly brown.

To Serve:

Serve with green chutney and onion rings.

Murgh Navrattan Korma

A rich curry garnished with dried fruits!

Serves: 4-5　　　　Preparation time: 15 minutes　　　　Cooking time: 40 minutes

Ingredients:

Chicken boneless or chicken with bone, cut into 8 pieces	1 kg
Almond paste	100 gms/½ cup
Bay leaf (tej patta)	1
Butter, unsalted	25 gms/5 tsp
Cinnamon sticks	5
Cloves	6
Cream	120 ml/²/₃ cup
Garlic paste	30 gms/6 tsp
Ginger paste	30 gms/6 tsp
Green cardamoms	10
Green chillies, slit into half	6
Mace powder (javitri)	3 gms/²/₃ tsp
Onions, grated	180 gms/¾ cup
Red chilli powder	10 gms/2 tsp
Refined oil	25 ml/1²/₃ tbs
Salt to taste	

Turmeric powder (haldi)	5 gms/1 tsp
Vetivier (kewda)	3 drops
Yoghurt, whisked	20 gms/4 tsp

For garnishing:

Almonds	20 gms/4 tsp
Black cumin seed (shah jeera), roasted and powdered	3 gms/²/₃ tsp
Cashewnuts	20 gms/4 tsp
Fresh ginger juliennes	1 gm/¼ tsp
Fresh mint leaves	3 gms/²/₃ tsp
Hazelnuts	10 gms/2 tsp
Pistachios	15 gms/3 tsp
Raisins	10 gms/2 tsp
Saffron strands, dissolved in 15 ml of warm milk	3 gms/²/₃ tsp

Method:

Step 1. Fry the pistachios, cashewnuts, hazelnuts and almonds in a little butter for the garnish and keep aside.

2. Heat the oil and butter in the same pan. Add the bay leaf, cinnamon sticks, cloves and cardamoms, and sauté over medium heat until the spices begins to crackle. the ginger and garlic pastes, and whisked yoghurt, and cook separates from the mixture.

3. Add the onions, and sauté for few minutes. Add turmeric and red chilli powder, almond paste, salt over medium heat for 5-10 minutes until the oil heat for 20-25 minutes till the mace powder and

4. Add the chicken, stir and cook over medium chicken is cooked. Add cream, green chillies, few drops of vetivier.

To Serve:

Garnish with the sautéed nuts, raisins, ginger juliennes and saffron dissolved in milk. Sprinkle with cumin seed powder and mint leaves, and serve hot with steamed rice or rotis.

Murgh Navrattan Korma

Mur-muri Kebab

Tempting starters—chicken spring rolls

Serves: 4-5   Preparation time: 1 hour   Cooking time: 30 minutes

Ingredients:

For the stuffing:

Chicken, boneless	
(cut into 1.25 cm X 1.25 cm or ½" X ½")	500 gms
Cottage cheese (paneer), grated	50 gms/¼ cup
Garam masala	10 gms/2 tsp
Ginger, chopped	30 gms/2 tbs
Green chillies, chopped	10 gms/2 tsp
Green coriander, chopped	10 gms/2 tsp
Lemon juice	20 ml/1⅓ tbs
Oil	30 ml/2 tbs
Onions, chopped	50 gms/¼ cup
Salt to taste	
White pepper powder	5 gms/1 tsp

For the romali rotis (6):

Eggs, beaten	2
Flour	250 gms/1¼ cups
Milk	200 ml/1 cup
Oil	50 gms/3⅓ tbs
Oil for deep frying	500 ml/2½ cups
Salt to taste	
Sugar	3 gms/⅔ tsp

Method:

Step 1. **For the stuffing:** Heat the oil in a pan, add the ginger and onions and sauté over medium heat for 30 seconds.

2. Add the chicken, white pepper powder, garam masala, green chillies and green coriander and cook on low heat stirring occasionally. When the chicken is cooked add the paneer, salt and lemon juice.

3. **For the romali rotis:** Seive flour. Make a depression in the centre and pour the milk, sugar, salt, oil and the beaten eggs.

4. Mix gradually to make a soft dough. Cover with a moist cloth and keep aside for half an hour. Knead the dough again. Make 6 balls, dust with flour, cover and keep aside for 15 minutes.

5. Flatten each ball between the palms and roll into thin 24 cm or 12"-round discs.

6. Preheat the oven to 175 °C (350 °F) and bake the rotis on a roasting tray for 3-4 minutes. Bake on both sides.

7. Cut each roti into 6 pieces. Stuff each roti piece with the stuffing, shape like a cigar and seal edges with water. Deep fry 10 pieces at a time.

To Serve:

Serve with cucumbers, tomatoes, sliced onions and mint chutney.

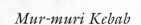

Mur-muri Kebab

Dum ka Murgh

Chicken cooked gently in its own juices!

Serves: 4-5   Preparation time: 15 minutes   Cooking time: 30 minutes

Ingredients:

Chicken (small, boneless cubes)	1 kg	Green chillies, slit into half	6
Almond paste	100 gms/½ cup	Mace powder (javitri)	3 gms/²/₃ tsp
Bay leaf (tej patta)	1	Mint leaves, fresh	5 gms/1 tsp
Butter, unsalted	25 gms/5 tsp	Oil	25 ml/1²/₃ tbs
Cinnamon sticks	5	Onions, grated	180 gms/¾ cup
Cloves	6	Red chilli powder	10 gms/2 tsp
Cream	120 ml/²/₃ cup	Salt to taste	
Garlic paste	25 gms/5 tsp	Turmeric powder (haldi)	5 gms/1 tsp
Ginger paste	25 gms/5 tsp	Vetivier (kewda)	3 drops
Green cardamoms	10		

Method:

Step 1. Heat the oil and butter in a pan. Add bay leaf, cinnamon, cloves and cardamoms and sauté over medium heat until they begin to crackle.

2. Add the onions and sauté for few minutes. Add the ginger and garlic pastes, turmeric, red chilli powder, salt and almond paste and cook over medium heat for 5-10 minutes until the oil separates from the mixture.

3. Add the chicken, stir and cook over medium heat for 10-15 minutes.

4. Add the cream, green chillies, mace powder and vetivier.

5. Sprinkle with fresh mint leaves, cover and seal lid with a dough. Let the chicken simmer over very low heat for 5-6 minutes. [It could also be kept in a preheated slow oven to 120°C (240°F) for 10 minutes. This is *dum* cooking.]

To Serve:

Serve hot with rotis or naan.

Bara Boti Kebab 30

Lamb Do Piaza 36

Malai Seekh Kebab 28

Safed Maas 43

Ghule Kebab 28

Rara Gosht 30

Lamb

Raan Musallam

Roast leg of lamb

Serves: 4-5   Preparation time: 2½ hours   Cooking time: 3½ hours

Ingredients:

Leg of lamb (*raan*)	1 kg	Green cardamoms	6
Almonds, blanched	4	Green coriander, chopped	10 gms/2 tsp
Aniseed	10 gms/2 tsp	Mace (javitri)	10 gms/2 tsp
Asafoetida (heeng), crushed	2 gms/½ tsp	Nutmeg (jaiphal)	1
Bay leaves (tej patta)	4	Oil	200 ml/1 cup
Black cardamoms	3	Onion, medium	1
Cinnamon sticks	3	Poppy seeds, soaked	9 gms/1¾ tsp
Cloves	4	Red chilli powder	10 gms/2 tsp
Coconut, desiccated	10 gms/2 tsp	Salt to taste	
Fresh mint	10 gms/2 tsp	Yoghurt	50 gms/3⅓ tbs
Ginger	50 gms/3⅓ tbs		

Method:

Step 1. Remove all the white membrane from the surface of the lamb. Prick repeatedly and thoroughly down to the bone, with a strong and large-pronged fork, until all the fibres are broken and the meat well-loosened. The success of this dish depends upon doing this well.

2. Grind together mace, nutmeg, cloves, cinnamon, black and green cardamoms, ginger, onion, salt, red chilli powder, poppy seeds and coconut. Apply the ground spices evenly all over the *raan* (leg) and prick again so that the spices soak into the body of the meat. Marinate for 2 hours.

3. Tie the *raan* with a string so that the meat stays on the bone whilst cooking. Place the *raan* in a large pan.

4. Cover with a mixture of oil, yoghurt, bay leaves and aniseed. Add 1 litre of water, cover and cook on moderate heat until water is reduced to 150 ml.

5. Add the crushed asafoetida in 3 tsp of water, add this to the raan and cook until 100 ml of gravy is left.

To Serve:

Serve hot garnished with almonds and green coriander.

Malai Seekh Kebab

Minced lamb kebab, with herbs and cashewnuts, an extraordinary starter or cocktail snack

Serves: 4-5   Preparation time: 25 minutes   Cooking time: 15 minutes

Ingredients:

Lamb, minced	900 gms/4½ cups	Green coriander, finely chopped	20 gms/4 tsp
Butter for basting	50 gms/3⅓ tbs	Lamb kidney fat	150 gms/¾ cup
Cashewnut paste	75 gms/⅓ cup	Oil	50 ml/3⅓ tbs
Eggs, whisked	2	Onions, finely chopped	40 gms/2⅔ tbs
Garam masala	10 gms/2 tsp	Salt to taste	
Ginger, finely chopped	40 gms/2⅔ tbs	White pepper powder	3 gms/⅔ tsp
Green chillies, finely chopped	8		

Method:

Step 1. Add all the ingredients, except butter, to the lamb mince and mix well. Keep aside for 15 minutes.
     2. Divide into 12 equal portions and make into balls.
     3. Preheat the tandoor or oven to 160 °C (320 °F). To make the seekh kebab, spear the skewer through each ball. Spread by pressing each ball with a moistened palm along the length of the skewers, until each kebab is 8-10 cm long and about 4 cm apart.
     4. Roast in a tandoor or charcoal grill or preheated oven for 8-10 minutes.
     5. Remove and hang the skewers to let the excess moisture drip off.
     6. Baste with butter and roast again for 2 minutes.

To Serve:

Remove the kebabs from the skewers on to a platter and garnish with onion rings, lemon wedges and shredded cabbage or carrots.

Ghule Kebab

Golden fried lamb kebabs

Serves: 4-5   Preparation time: 2½ hours   Cooking time: 15 minutes

Ingredients:

Lamb, minced	600 gms/3 cups	Red chilli powder	4 gms/¾ tsp
Black cumin (shah jeera)	2 gms/½ tsp	Salt to taste	
Coriander powder	4 gms/¾ tsp		
Eggs, beaten	2	**For the filling:**	
Garam masala	4 gms/¾ tsp	Cottage cheese (paneer), grated	50 gms/3⅓ tbs
Ginger paste	10 gms/2 tsp	Green cardamom powder	2 gms/½ tsp
Gram flour (besan)	25 gms/5 tsp	Green chillies, finely chopped	10 gms/2 tsp
Green cardamom powder	2 gms/½ tsp	Khoya (dried milk), grated	50 gms/3⅓ tbs
Green chilli, finely minced	10 gms/2 tsp	Lemon juice	5 ml/1 tsp
Green coriander, chopped	10 gms/2 tsp	Maize flour (makke ka atta)	2 gms/½ tsp
Lamb fat, minced	100 gms/½ cup	Milk	15 ml/1 tbs
Lemon juice	10 ml/2 tsp	Onions, fried golden brown	150 gms/¾ cup
Oil for deep frying	500 ml/2½ cups	Saffron	1 gm
Onions, grated	25 gms/5 tsp	Salt to taste	
Pomegranate juice	30 ml/2 tbs	Yellow chilli powder	2 gms/½ tsp

Method:

Step 1. Combine lamb mince, lamb fat, salt, lemon juice, coriander powder, red chilli powder, black cumin, garam masala, green cardamom powder, onions, green chillies, green coriander and ginger.
     2. Mince twice, very finely and keep in the refrigerator for 2 hours till mince gets chilled.

Bhopali Seekh Kebab

3. In a bowl combine the mince mixture and beaten eggs, and mix thoroughly. Add the gram flour and pomegranate juice. Check the salt.
4. Divide into 15 equal portions, roll into balls and keep in the refrigerator.
5. In a bowl mix the ingredients for the filling, check the salt and divide into 15 equal portions.
6. Fill each mince ball with a portion of stuffing and shape into a pear-shaped.
7. Heat the oil in deep vessel/*kadhai* over medium heat. Deep fry 5 pieces at a time until crisp and golden.

To Serve:

Serve hot with fresh mint chutney and green salad.

Bhopali Seekh Kebab

Skewered minced lamb kebabs

Serves: 4-5   Preparation time: 25 minutes   Cooking time: 15 minutes

Ingredients:

Lamb, minced	900 gms/4½ cups	Green chilli, finely chopped	8 gms/1²/₃ tsp
Green coriander, finely chopped	10 gms/2 tsp	Lamb kidney fat	150 gms/¾ cup
Butter to baste	50 gms/3¹/₃ tbs	Mace powder (javitri)	5 gms/1 tsp
Cardamom powder	3 gms/²/₃ tsp	Onion paste, browned	100 gms/½ cup
Cottage cheese (paneer), grated	15 gms/3 tsp	Poppy seed paste	100 gms/½ cup
Garam masala	20 gms/4 tsp	Salt to taste	
Ginger paste	40 gms/2²/₃ tbs		

Method:

Step 1. Combine all the ingredients in a bowl, mix thoroughly and refrigerate for 15 minutes.
2. Divide into 20 equal portions and make into balls.
3. Preheat oven to 175 °C (350 °F).
4. Spear each meatball with the skewer. Spread by pressing each along the length of the skewer with a wet hand, making each kebab 8-10 cms long, 4 cms apart.
5. Roast in the hot tandoor or oven or charcoal grill for 8-10 minutes.
6. Remove and hang the skewers to let the excess moisture drip off.
7. Baste with butter and roast for another 2 minutes.

To Serve:

Garnish with sliced cucumbers, tomatoes and onion rings, and serve with fresh mint chutney.

Bara Boti Kebab

Boneless cubed lamb kebabs

Serves: 4-5   Preparation time: 3½ hours   Cooking time: 20 minutes

Ingredients:

Lamb cubes, boneless	1 kg	Oil	70 ml/4²/₃ tbs
Black pepper, crushed	6 gms/1¹/₃ tsp	Raw papaya paste (optional)	60 gms/4 tbs
Butter for basting	50 gms/3¹/₃ tbs	Red chilli powder	10 gms/2 tsp
Cheese, grated	70 gms/4²/₃ tbs	Saffron	2 gms
Cumin powder (jeera)	5 gms/1 tsp	Salt to taste	
Garam masala	15 gms/3 tsp	Vinegar	45 ml/3 tbs
Garlic paste	40 gms/2²/₃ tbs	Yoghurt, hung	200 gms/1 cup
Ginger paste	50 gms/3¹/₃ tbs		

Method:

Step 1. Make a marinade with 4 tbs oil, vinegar, ginger and garlic paste, salt, red chilli powder, black pepper and papaya.
2. Marinate the lamb in the paste for 2½ hours.
3. Mix together the yoghurt, 1 tbs of oil, cheese, garam masala, cumin powder and saffron.
4. Add this to the lamb mixture and marinate it for 1 hour.
5. Thread the lamb pieces onto skewers, 3 cms apart.
6. Cook in a moderate tandoor/oven to 175 ºC (350 ºF) for 15 minutes or on a charcoal grill for 10-12 minutes.
7. Brush with butter and cook for another 3-4 minutes.

To Serve:

Remove from skewers, serve on a bed of lettuce and green salad, accompanied with any Indian bread and mint chutney.

Rara Gosht

A simple yet delicious lamb curry

Serves: 4-5   Preparation time: 2½ hours
Cooking time: 35 minutes

Ingredients:

Lamb from the shoulder, cubed	1 kg
Cumin seed (jeera)	5 gms/1 tsp
Fresh red chillies	8
Garam masala	5 gms/1 tsp
Garlic, chopped	12 gms/2½ tsp
Ginger, chopped	12 gms/2½ tsp
Green cardamom	4
Green chillies	6
Green coriander, chopped	15 gms/3 tsp
Hot water	200 ml/1 cup
Oil	100 ml/½ cup
Onions, chopped	400 gms/2 cups
Salt to taste	
Tomatoes, chopped	20 gms/4 tsp
Yoghurt	200 gms/1 cup

Method:

Step 1. Clean lamb and marinate yoghurt mixed with the garlic, ginger and salt. Keep aside for 2 hours.
2. Heat the oil. Add the cumin seed, cardamom and red chillies, and sauté for 30 seconds.

3. Add the onions and cook until golden brown then add tomatoes and cook for 5 minutes.
4. To this, add the lamb and the marinade, and cook until the oil separates from the gravy. Add 1 cup of hot water, garam masala, cover and simmer on low heat until lamb is completely cooked.

To Serve:

Serve hot, garnished with coriander leaves and sliced chillies.

Gosht Chaap Achari

Lamb chops cooked with whole spices

Serves: 4-5   Preparation time: 2½ hours   Cooking time: 30 minutes

Ingredients:

Lamb chops, on 2 bones	8 pieces	Lemon juice	15 ml/1 tbs
Aniseed	5 gms/1 tsp	Mustard oil (sarson ka tel)	50 ml/3⅓ tbs
Black cardamom	2 gms/½ tsp	Mustard seeds (raee)	5 gms/1 tsp
Black pepper	5 gms/1 tsp	Onion seeds (kalonji)	5 gms/1 tsp
Chaat masala	5 gms/1 tsp	Raw papaya, a small piece or meat tenderizer	
Cloves	3 gms/⅔ tsp	Red chilli powder	15 gms/3 tsp
Garlic paste	10 gms/2 tsp	Salt to taste	
Ginger paste	10 gms/2 tsp	Yoghurt, whisked	50 gms/¼ cup
Gram flour (besan)	10 gms/2 tsp		

Method:

Step 1. Flatten the chops with a steak hammer.
2. Rub the chops with the papaya, ginger and garlic pastes and salt and keep aside.
3. Heat the gram flour in a pan till light brown and sprinkle over the lamb chops.
4. To the yoghurt add the remaining ingredients and mix well to a fine batter. (Do not add chaat masala or lemon juice.)
5. Marinate the chops in this marinade for 2 hours.
6. Preheat the oven to 175 °C (350 °F).
7. Skewer the chops and roast in a hot tandoor or oven until cooked.

To Serve:

Remove the chops from the skewer. Sprinkle with chaat masala and lemon juice and serve.

Gosht Chaap Achari

Tandoori Raan

Spring lamb leg cooked in spiced yoghurt

Serves: 4-5   Preparation time: 4-7 hours   Cooking time: 1 hour

Ingredients:

Legs of lamb	2	Mace powder (javitri)	3 gms/²/₃ tsp
Almonds, skinned, blanched,		Nutmeg powder (jaiphal)	3 gms/²/₃ tsp
sliced, fried golden	30 gms/2 tbs	Onion paste	120 gms/²/₃ cup
Aniseed	3 gms/²/₃ tsp	Poppy seed paste	100 gms/¹/₂ cup
Bay leaves (tej patta)	2	Red chilli powder	10 gms/2 tsp
Butter	30 gms/2 tbs	Refined oil	30 ml/2 tbs
Cinnamon powder	3 gms/²/₃ tsp	Saffron	1 gm
Cinnamon	4	Salt to taste	
Clove powder	5 gms/1 tsp	Small cardamom powder	5 gms/1 tsp
Fresh coconut paste	120 gms/²/₃ cup	Vetivier (kewda)	3 drops
Garlic paste	50 gms/3¹/₃ tbs	White pepper	20 gms/4 tsp
Ginger paste	50 gms/3¹/₃ tbs	Yoghurt, whisked	120 gms/²/₃ cup
Green coriander	10 gms/2 tsp		

Method:

Step 1. Remove all the white membranes from the surface of the lamb. Prick it with a fork repeatedly and very thoroughly, down to the bone, until the fibers are broken and the meat well loosened. The success of this special dish depends upon how well this is done.

2. In a bowl, combine the poppy seed paste, coconut paste, onion paste, ginger and garlic pastes, red chilli powder, clove powder, cinnamon powder and yoghurt and whisk to a fine batter. Add salt to taste. Rub the paste over the lamb leg and let it stand for at least 3 hours or preferably, overnight.

3. Skewer each leg separately and roast in a slow tandoor for at least 30-45 minutes. Remove, baste with butter and roast for a further 15 minutes or till done.

4. Remove from the skewers.

To Serve:

Serve with sliced cucumber, sliced onions, sliced tomatoes, lemon wedges, chaat masala and fresh mint chutney. Recommended with hot naan.

Tandoori Raan

Kareli Kebab

Lamb shanks stewed with cinnamon flavour

Serves: 4-5   Preparation time: 2 hours   Cooking time: 1 hour

Ingredients:

Lamb, shanks on the bone, 10 cm long karelis	1 kg	Green cardamoms	10
Bay leaves (tej patta)	2	Maize flour (makke ka atta)	3 gms/²/₃ tsp
Cinnamon sticks	4	Oil	60 ml/4 tbs
Garam masala	15 gms/3 tsp	Red chilli powder	10 gms/2 tsp
Garlic paste	50 gms/3¹/₃ tbs	Salt to taste	
Ginger paste	50 gms/3¹/₃ tbs		

Method:

Step 1. Remove all the white membranes from the surface of the lamb. Prick repeatedly and very thoroughly down to the bone with a large fork until all the fibres are broken. The success of the dish depends upon how well this is done.

2. Apply the ginger and garlic paste, the red chilli powder, salt, maize flour and garam masala evenly all over the shanks. Let them rest in this marinade for at least 1-2 hours.

3. Heat the oil in a pan and add all the whole spices. Sauté over medium heat until they begin to crackle.

4. Arrange the shanks in the pan and sauté over medium heat for 10-15 minutes until the meat changes colour.

5. Add 400 ml (2 cups) of hot water, stir and cover. Let the meat simmer for 40 minutes or until it is completely tender.

6. Remove each piece with a tong and keep aside.

7. Strain the sauce and reduce further on very low heat until it becomes a thick concentrate (about 200-50 ml).

8. Add shanks to the sauce, coating each one evenly.

To Serve:

Serve garnished with sliced cucumbers, onion rings, tomatoes and lemon wedges.

Nilgiri Korma

Lamb cooked in a coconut curry

Serves: 4-5   Preparation time: 15 minutes   Cooking time: 1 hour

Ingredients:

Lamb cubes, boneless	1 kg	Garlic paste	40 gms/2²/₃ tbs
Bay leaf (tej patta)	1	Ginger paste	40 gms/2²/₃ tbs
Cinnamon sticks	5	Green cardamoms	8
Cloves	8	Green coriander, chopped	20 gms/4 tsp
Coriander seed	50 gms/3¹/₃ tbs	Onion paste	200 gms/1 cup
Cumin seed (jeera)	15 gms/3 tsp	Poppy seed	10 gms/2 tsp
Fennel seed (saunf)	10 gms/2 tbs	Red chillies	20
Fresh coconut, grated	500 gms/2½ cups	Refined oil	100 ml/½ cup
Fresh mint, chopped	20 gms/4 tsp	Salt to taste	

Method:

Step 1. Dry roast the coriander seeds, cumin seeds, fennel seeds, poppy seeds and red chillies, and grind to a fine paste using 50-60 ml of water.

2. Heat the oil in a pan, add the cinnamon sticks, cloves, cardamoms and bay leaf, and sauté over medium heat, until they begin to crackle. Add the onion paste, garlic and ginger paste and cook for 5-6 minutes.

3. In a separate pan heat 2 cups of water, add the lamb cubes, bring it to a slow boil and cook for 10 minutes.

4. Add the boiled lamb to the sautéed spices and salt to taste. Cook over medium heat for 10-15 minutes, stirring constantly.

5. Add a cup of hot water, cover and cook on low heat until lamb is almost cooked.

6. Grind the grated coconut in a liquidizer to a very fine paste. Add 150 ml of hot water to the coconut paste and strain through a fine cheese cloth to get thick, fresh coconut milk.

7. Add the coconut milk to the lamb, uncover and cook for 10 minutes, until the gravy thickens.

To Serve:

Sprinkle with chopped green coriander and mint.

Gosht Shahi Korma

Lamb curried with yoghurt, dried milk, cream and almonds

Serves: 4-5   Preparation time: 1 hour   Cooking time: 30 minutes

Ingredients:

Lamb, boneless	1 kg	Green cardamoms	10
Almond (badam) paste	50 gms/¼ cup	Green chillies	50 gms/6-10
Bay leaves (tej patta)	2	Khoya (dried milk)	50 gms/¼ cup
Cinnamon sticks	5	Onions, sliced	150 gms/¾ cup
Cream	100 ml/½ cup	Salt to taste	
Garlic paste	25 gms/5 tsp	Varq (silver leaf)	2
Ghee (clarified butter)	150 gms/¾ cup	White butter	100 gms/½ cup
Ginger paste	25 gms/5 tsp	White pepper powder	2 gms/½ tsp
Green cardamom powder	2 gms/½ tsp	Yoghurt	250 gms/1¼ cup

Method:

Step 1. Wash and dry the lamb and cut into small cubes.
  2. Rub the ginger and garlic pastes over the lamb and keep aside for 1 hour.
  3. Heat the ghee and white butter. Add bay leaves, cinnamon sticks and cardamoms till they crackle, then add onions and sauté till soft.
  4. Add the cubed lamb and cook over high heat until the lamb changes colour.
  5. Add the yoghurt and almond paste and cook on low heat for another 25 minutes or until the lamb cubes are tender. Season to taste with cream, green chillies, white pepper powder, salt and green cardamom powder.

To Serve:

Serve garnished with grated khoya and silver leaves, accompanied by roti or **Zafrani Pulao** (see page 89).

Kohe Awadh

A lamb curry with a difference

Serves: 4-5   Preparation time: 15 minutes
          Cooking time: 3 hours

Ingredients:

Lamb meat from the shanks, on the bone, kareli	1 kg/10 pieces
Bay leaves (tej patta)	2
Black pepper powder	5 gms/1 tsp
Cinnamon sticks	2
Cloves	8
Cumin powder (jeera)	1 gm/¹⁄₅ tsp
Garlic paste	40 gms/2²⁄₃ tbs
Ghee (clarified butter)	60 ml/¹⁄₃ cup
Ginger juliennes	10 gms/2 tsp
Ginger paste	40 gms/2²⁄₃ tbs
Green cardamoms	8
Green cardamom powder	1 gm/¹⁄₅ tsp
Green coriander, chopped	5 gms/1 tsp
Kashmiri red chilli powder	5 gms/1 tsp
Mace powder (javitri)	5 gms/1 tsp

Gosht Shahi Korma

Milk	15 ml/1 tbs	Salt to taste	
Onions	175 gms/¾ cup	Vetivier (kewda)	2 drops
Saffron	5 gms/1 tsp	Yoghurt	400 gms/2 cups

Method:

Step 1. Fry the onions in a little ghee, grind to a paste, and keep aside.

2. In the same pan, heat the rest of the ghee and add the meat, green cardamoms, cloves, cinnamon, bay leaves, ginger and garlic paste, and salt. Cover and cook on low heat for 30 minutes. Stir occasionally. Uncover and stir fry for a few minutes until the liquid evaporates.

3. Add the yoghurt and continue to stir fry till the liquid evaporates again.

4. Add the red chilli powder, dissolved in 30 ml of water, and stir for a minute. Add the fried onion paste dissolved in 3 tbs of water and continue to fry. Add a tablespoon of water when the liquid evaporates, to ensure that the sauce and lamb do not burn.

5. Add half the pepper and cumin and 6 cups of water and bring to a boil. Cover, lower the heat, seal the lid with dough and simmer on *dum* for at least 1 hour.

6. Unseal and remove the lamb from the gravy. Strain the gravy, return to the stove and reduce the gravy to pouring consistency.

7. Add the mace, cardamom powder and the saffron with kewda mixed in milk. Cook for about 5 minutes.

To Serve:

To serve, pour the sauce over the kareli and garnish with ginger juliennes and green coriander.

Gosht Gulfam

Lamb with cottage cheese

Serves: 4-5   Preparation time: 15 minutes   Cooking time: 1 hour

Ingredients:

Lamb (shoulder or leg)	1 kg	Green coriander, chopped	15 gms/3 tsp
Almonds	25 gms/5 tsp	Mace powder (javitri)	3 gms/⅔ tsp
Bay leaves (tej patta)	2	Morels (guchchi), dried mushrooms	20 gms/4 tsp
Cardamom powder	5 gms/1 tsp	Oil	80 ml/5⅓ tbs
Cinnamon powder	5 gms/1 tsp	Onion paste	100 gms/½ cup
Cottage cheese (paneer), grated	100 gms/½ cup	Pistachios, blanched, skinned and halved	50 gms/¼ cup
Cream	30 ml/2 tbs	Red chilli powder	12 gms/2½ tsp
Cumin powder (jeera)	10 gms/2 tsp	Salt to taste	
Garam masala	10 gms/2 tsp	Tomatoes, diced	100 gms/½ cup
Garlic paste	40 gms/2⅔ tbs	Water/chicken stock	300-400 ml/1½-2 cups
Ginger paste	40 gms/2⅔ tbs	White pepper powder	10 gms/2 tsp
Green chillies, slit	10 gms/8		

Method:

Step 1. Debone the leg or shoulder, spread and flatten the meat completely.

2. In a bowl mix to a paste the grated paneer, almonds, pistachios, morels, salt, pepper, half the red chilli powder, half the garam masala, half the ginger and garlic pastes, and the cream.

3. Spread the paste on the lamb evenly. Roll the lamb like a swiss roll, and tie it firmly using kitchen thread.

4. Place the lamb on a roasting tray, sprinkle over with salt, a pinch of garam masala, a pinch of chilli powder, oil, crushed bay leaves, the cardamom and cinnamon powder and add 300-400 ml (1½-2 cups) water or chicken stock.

5. Cook in a preheated oven to 175 ºC (350 ºF) for 45 minutes, basting every 15-20 minutes with the drippings.

6. When the lamb is completely cooked, strain the gravy from the roasting pan. Cook the gravy on low heat till it is reduced to a semi-thick rich sauce (about 120 ml/⅔ cup).

7. Heat the oil in a pan, add onions, the remaining ginger and garlic pastes, diced tomatoes, garam masala, mace powder, salt, green chillies, cumin powder and green coriander, the sauce, and cook for 2-3 minutes. Keep it hot.

To Serve:

Untie the lamb, cut into thick slices and arrange on a serving dish. Pour the hot sauce over the meat and serve immediately.
Note: While rolling the meat, a hard boiled egg can be placed in the centre.

Lamb Rogan Josh

A mild Kashmiri lamb dish

Serves: 4-5   Preparation time: 15 minutes   Cooking time: 35 minutes

Ingredients:

Lamb (preferably chops)	1 kg	Onions, chopped	180 gms/¾ cups
Bay leaves (tej patta)	3	Red chilli powder	10 gms/2 tsp
Black cumin seeds (shah jeera)	2 gms/½ tsp	Refined oil	60 ml/4 tbs
Cinnamon sticks	2	Salt to taste	
Cloves	10	Sugar	5 gms/1 tsp
Fennel seed powder (saunf)	5 gms/1 tsp	Tomatoes, skinned, deseeded	
Ginger paste	10 gms/2 tsp	and chopped	400 gms/2 cups
Green cardamoms	8	Water/ lamb stock	200 ml/1 cup

Method:

Step 1. Clean lamb chops and remove excess fat. Pat with a paper towel, sprinkle with salt, and keep aside for 10 minutes.

2. Heat the oil, add sugar, cloves, bay leaves, green cardamoms and cinnamon sticks and sauté for 2-3 minutes.

3. Add the lamb chops and cook over medium heat until the lamb chops are lightly browned.

4. Add the chopped onions and sauté till browned.

5. Add red chilli powder, black cumin seeds, chopped tomatoes and ginger paste and fry till oil separates from the gravy.

6. Add the water/stock and cook until the chops are tender. Add fennel seed powder. Cover and simmer for 10 minutes on a low fire.

To Serve:

Serve garnished with a pinch of fennel seed powder, with steamed rice or roti.

Lamb Do Piaza

Lamb curry with lots of onions, added twice, hence 'do piaza'!

Serves: 4-5   Preparation time: 15 minutes
Cooking time: 45 minutes

Ingredients:

Lamb, cubed	1 kg
Bay leaves (tej patta)	3
Black pepper crushed	10 gms/2 tsp
Button onions	300 gms/1½ cups
Butter	20 gms/1⅓ tbs
Cinnamon sticks	5
Cloves	10
Coriander powder	10 gms/2 tsp
Cumin powder (jeera)	6 gms/1⅓ tsp
Garam masala	12 gms/2½ tsp
Garlic paste	60 gms/4 tbs
Ginger juliennes	6 gms/1⅓ tsp
Ginger paste	60 gms/4 tbs
Green cardamom pods	10
Green coriander, chopped	5 gms/1 tsp
Mace powder (javitri)	3 gms/⅔ tsp
Nutmeg powder (jaiphal)	½ nutmeg
Onions, chopped or sliced	200 gms/1 cup
Red chillies, whole	10 gms/8
Refined oil	100 ml/1 cup
Salt to taste	

| Tomatoes, skinned, deseeded and chopped | 300 gms/1½ cups | Turmeric powder (haldi) | 6 gms/1⅓ tsp |

Method:

Step 1. Blanch the button onions and toss in hot butter for a few minutes.
2. Heat the oil in a pan, add the turmeric and the whole spices (bay leaves, cloves, cinnamon sticks, whole red chillies, and cardamoms) and sauté over medium heat for few seconds until they begin to crackle.
3. Add the onions and sauté until soft and golden in colour. Add the ginger and garlic pastes and chopped tomatoes, stir and cook for 5 minutes.
4. Then add the lamb, stir and cook for 10-15 minutes over medium heat until a pleasant aroma comes from the lamb. Reduce heat, simmer on a low fire and cook until the lamb is tender.
5. Sprinkle with garam masala, coriander powder, cumin powder, mace powder, nutmeg powder and black pepper powder. Adjust the salt. Add the button onions, stir, cover and cook for 2-3 minutes.

To Serve

Serve sprinkled with green coriander and ginger juliennes.

Lamb Chilli Fry

A quick stir fried lamb delicacy

Serves: 4-5   Preparation time: 5 hours   Cooking time: 45 minutes

Ingredients:

Lamb, cleaned, washed and sliced	900 gms	Green coriander, chopped	10 gms/2 tsp
Cumin, roasted and powdered (jeera)	5 gms/1 tsp	Lemon juice	30 ml/2 tbs
Garlic paste	50 gms/3⅓ tbs	Oil	100 ml/½ cup
Ginger paste	50 gms/3⅓ tbs	Onion rings or spring onions	200 gms/1 cup
Green and red chillies, slit in half	50 gms each	Red chilli powder	10 gms/2 tsp
		Salt for seasoning	
		Turmeric powder (haldi)	10 gms/2 tsp
		Water or stock	100 ml/½ cup

Method:

Step 1. Mix together the ginger and garlic pastes, turmeric powder, red chilli powder, salt and 3 tbs of oil.
2. Marinate the lamb in this mixture for at least 4-5 hours or, preferably, overnight.
3. Heat the oil in a *kadhai*/wok to smoking point. Put the marinated lamb into the wok, stir fry on a high heat for 4-5 minutes.
4. Sprinkle half a cup of water or stock on the lamb, stirring once or twice. Add the red and green chillies and onions rings, stir and cook for 2-3 minutes.
5. Season to taste with salt and lemon juice. Sprinkle with roasted cumin powder.

To Serve:

Serve garnished with green coriander, with raita and rotis.

Lamb Rogan Josh

Nahari Gosht

A favourite of the Nawabs of Lucknow

Serves: 4-5   Preparation time: 15 minutes   Cooking time: 45 minutes

Ingredients:

Lamb with bone (any cut)	1 kg	Green coriander, chopped	15 gms/3 tsp
Bay leaves (tej patta)	2	Lemon juice	10 ml/2 tsp
Black pepper	20	Mace (javitri)	3 gms/²⁄₃ tsp
Cinnamon sticks	4	Mustard oil (sarson ka tel)	150 ml/½ cup
Cloves	10	Onions, chopped	250 gms/1¼ cups
Coriander powder	20 gms/4 tsp	Onions, sliced	250 gms/1¼ cups
Fennel powder (saunf)	4 gms/¾ tsp	Red chillies	10 gms/8
Flour	4 gms/¾ tsp	Saffron	1 gm
Garam masala	10 gms/2 tsp	Salt to taste	
Garlic paste	5 gms/1 tsp	Turmeric powder (haldi)	10 gms/2 tsp
Ginger paste	5 gms/1 tsp	Vetivier (kewda)	1 tbs
Gram flour (besan)	4 gms/¾ tsp	Yoghurt, whisked	200 gms/1 cup
Green cardamoms	10		

Method:

Step 1. Clean and cut lamb into small pieces with the bone.

2. Heat 100 ml (½ cup) oil in a *kadhai*/wok, add the sliced onions and sauté over medium heat until golden brown.

3. Add the lamb, chopped onions, green cardamoms, cloves, cinnamon black pepper and bay leaves and cook until the liquid evaporates.

4. Add coriander powder, red chillies, turmeric, ginger and garlic pastes and salt and cook until the oil separates from the mixture.

5. Add the yoghurt, bring to a boil, reduce to medium heat and cook for 10 minutes.

6. Add 1 litre water and bring to a boil again. Cover and simmer, stirring occasionally, until lamb is tender.

7. Remove the meat from the gravy and keep aside.

8. Heat 3 tbs of the oil in a pan, add the flour and gram flour and cook over low heat, stirring constantly, until light brown. Add the gravy and stir.

9. Pass the thickened gravy through a soup strainer, return to the fire and bring to a boil.

10. Add the lamb, garam masala, fennel powder, lemon juice, vetivier, saffron and the mace, and stir.

To Serve:

Serve garnished with green coriander leaves with roti or naan.

Nahari Gosht

Bhuna Gosht

Fennel flavoured lamb curry

Serves: 4-5   Preparation time: 15 minutes   Cooking time: 45 minutes

Ingredients:

Lamb (leg and/or shoulder)	1 kg		
Bay leaves (tej patta)	3	Cumin powder (jeera)	8 gms/1²⁄₃ tsp
Black cumin powder (shah jeera)	5 gms/1 tsp	Fennel powder (saunf)	5 gms/1 tsp
Black pepper powder	5 gms/1 tsp	Garam masala	15 gms/3 tsp
Cinnamon sticks	5	Garlic paste	50 gms/3¹⁄₃ tbs
Cloves	10	Ginger juliennes	6 gms/1¹⁄₃ tsp

Ginger paste	50 gms/3¹⁄₃ tbs	Mace powder (javitri)	4 gms/¾ tsp
Green cardamoms	10	Oil	80 ml/¹⁄₃ cup
Green chillies, finely chopped	5	Onions, chopped	400 gms/2 cups
Green coriander, finely chopped	15 gms/3 tsp	Salt for seasoning	

Method:

Step 1. Roast the whole spices (cinnamon sticks, cloves and cardamoms) lightly over medium heat and grind.

2. Heat the oil in a pan, add the bay leaves and onions and sauté over medium heat until the onions are light golden.

3. Add the ginger and garlic pastes and black pepper powder, stir and cook for 2-3 minutes. Add the garam masala and cook for another 30 seconds.

4. Add the lamb cubes, and stir and cook for 20-25 minutes over medium heat until the lamb is tender.

5. Sprinkle with the ground whole spices. Season to taste with salt, mace powder, fennel powder and green chillies.

To Serve:

Serve garnished with green coriander and ginger juliennes.

Note: The lamb should be coated with thick brown gravy. It should not be of running consistency. The same dish could be made with tender lamb chops instead of lamb cubes.

Khada Masala Gosht

Hot and spicy lamb with whole spices

Serves: 4-5 **Preparation time: 15 minutes** **Cooking time: 45 minutes**

Ingredients:

Lamb, cubes	1 kg	Cumin powder (jeera)	6 gms/1¹⁄₃ tsp
Bay leaves (tej patta)	3	Fresh mint leaves, chopped	8 gms/1²⁄₃ tsp
Black pepper, crushed	10 gms/2 tsp	Garam masala	2 gms/½ tsp
Cinnamon sticks	5	Garlic paste	60 gms/4 tbs
Cloves	10	Ginger paste	60 gms/4 tbs
Coriander powder	10 gms/2 tsp	Green cardamoms	10
		Green chillies, whole	12
		Mace powder (javitri)	3 gms/²⁄₃ tsp
		Nutmeg powder (jaiphal)	½ nutmeg
		Oil	100 ml/½ cup
		Onions, chopped or sliced	200 gms/1 cup
		Red chillies, whole	10 gms/8
		Salt to taste	
		Yoghurt, whisked	200 gms/1 cup

Method:

Step 1. Heat the oil in a pan. Add the whole spices (bay leaves, cloves, cinnamon sticks, red chillies and cardamoms) and sauté over medium heat for few seconds until they begin to crackle.

2. Add the onions and sauté until soft and golden in colour. Add the ginger and garlic pastes, stir and cook for 5 minutes.

3. Add the lamb, stir and cook for 10-15 minutes over medium heat until the lamb emits a pleasant aroma.

4. Add yoghurt, stir and cook, for 5 minutes. Reduce heat, simmer and cook until the lamb is tender.

5. Sprinkle with garam masala, coriander powder, cumin powder, salt, mace powder, nutmeg powder and the crushed black pepper.

6. Arrange the green chillies over the cooked meat and cover the pan. Cook for 2-3 minutes.

To Serve:

Serve garnished with fresh mint leaves.

Khandari Gosht

Lamb marinated in pomegranate juice!

Serves: 4-5   Preparation time: 6-12 hours   Cooking time: 45 minutes

Ingredients:

Lamb cubes	1 kg	Green cardamoms	10
Almonds, fried	250 gms/1¼ cups	Mace powder (javitri)	3 gms/²/₃ tsp
Bay leaves (tej patta)	3	Milk	30 ml/2 tbs
Black pepper, crushed	10 gms/2 tsp	Nutmeg powder (jaiphal)	2 gms/½ tsp
Cinnamon sticks	5	Oil	100 ml/½ cup
Cloves	10	Onions, chopped or sliced	200 gms/1 cup
Coriander powder	10 gms/2 tsp	Pomegranate juice	250 ml/1¼ cups
Cumin powder (jeera)	6 gms/1¹/₃ tsp	Red chilli powder	10 gms/2 tsp
Fresh mint leaves, chopped	8 gms/1²/₃ tsp	Saffron	0.5 gms
Garam masala	2 gms/½ tsp	Salt to taste	
Garlic paste	60 gms/4 tbs	Yoghurt	200 gms/1 cup
Ginger paste	60 gms/4 tbs		

Method:

Step 1. Marinate the lamb in pomegranate juice for 6-12 hours.

2. Heat the oil in a pan, add whole spices (bay leaves, cloves, cinnamon sticks and cardamoms) and sauté over medium heat for a few seconds until they begin to crackle.

3. Add the onions, sauté until soft and golden in colour. Add ginger and garlic pastes and red chili powder, stir and cook for 5 minutes.

4. Add the marinated lamb with the marinade, stir and cook for 10-15 minutes over medium heat until a pleasant aroma comes from the lamb.

5. Add the yoghurt, stir and cook for 5 minutes. Reduce heat, simmer on low heat and cook until the lamb is tender.

6. Sprinkle with garam masala, coriander powder, cumin powder, mace, nutmeg, salt and crushed black pepper.

To Serve:

Transfer to a serving dish, sprinkle with saffron dissolved in a little milk, fried almonds and fresh mint leaves.

Dum Shahi Handi Kofta

An exotic meat ball curry with the added richness of dried apricots!

Serves: 4-5   Preparation time: 25 minutes   Cooking time: 30 minutes

Ingredients:

For the koftas:		For the gravy:	
Lamb (very finely minced)	1 kg	Bay leaves (tej patta)	2
Butter	50 gms/3¹/₃ tbs	Cinnamon sticks	3
Coriander powder	4 gms/¾ tsp	Cloves	10
Dried apricots, diced	150 gms/¾ cup	Cream	10 ml/2 tsp
Fennel powder (saunf)	4 gms/¾ tsp	Garam masala	10 gms/2 tsp
Garlic paste	25 gms/5 tsp	Garlic paste	50 gms/3¹/₃ tbs
Ginger paste	25 gms/5 tsp	Ginger paste	50 gms/3¹/₃ tbs
Green chillies, finely chopped	6 gms/2	Green cardamoms	10
Green coriander, finely chopped	10 gms/2 tsp	Green coriander, chopped	15 gms/3 tsp
Onions, grated	120 gms/²/₃ cup	Mace powder (javitri)	4 gms/¾ tsp
Salt for seasoning		Oil	80 ml/¹/₃ cup
White pepper powder	4 gms/¾ tsp	Onion paste	160 gms/¾ cup

Red chilli powder	10 gms/2 tsp	Tomatoes, skinned, deseeded	
Saffron strand, dissolved in 15 ml of milk	1 gm	and chopped	350 gms/1¾ cups
Salt for seasoning		Vetivier (kewda)	3 drops

Method:

Step 1. Mix all the ingredients for the koftas (meat balls)—except for the diced apricots—with the lamb mince using a wooden spoon. Mix thoroughly until the mixture sticks to the spoon. Season to taste with salt. Divide this mixture into 25 balls.

2. Stuff each meat ball with a little diced apricot.

3. Heat the oil in a pan, add the bay leaves, cloves, cardamoms and cinnamon sticks and sauté over medium heat for 30 seconds.

4. Add the onion paste, ginger and garlic pastes and sauté for 30 seconds. Add red chilli powder, stir and cook for 3-4 minutes. Add the chopped tomatoes, stir and cook.

5. Add the rest of the spices and simmer over medium heat until the oil separates from the tomato gravy.

6. Now add the koftas very carefully into the gravy. Add 1½ cups of hot water, sprinkle garam masala, cover the pan and simmer for 10 minutes.

7. Add cream, the saffron mixture, mace powder and vetivier and remove from the heat.

To Serve:

Serve the koftas with green coriander, accompanied with a vegetable preparation, raita and rotis or rice.

Hyderabadi Keema

The humble minced lamb transformed into a gourmet delight

Serves: 4-5   Preparation time: 20 minutes   Cooking time: 20 minutes

Ingredients:

Lamb, coarsely ground	1 kg	Green coriander, chopped	15 gms/3 tsp
Bay leaves (tej patta)	2	Green cardamoms	8
Black pepper, crushed	6 gms/1⅓ tsp	Green chillies, slit in half	10
Cinnamon sticks (4 cm pieces)	3	Mace powder (javitri)	3 gms/⅔ tsp
Cloves	10	Onions, diced	25 gms/5 tsp
Fresh mint leaves	10 gms/2 tsp	Red chilli powder	10 gms/2 tsp
Garam masala	10 gms/2 tsp	Refined oil	100 ml/½ cup
Garlic paste	50 gms/3⅓ tbs	Salt for seasoning	
Ginger, finely julienned	6 gms/1⅓ tsp	Yoghurt, whisked	100 gms/½ cup
Ginger paste	50 gms/3⅓ tbs		

Method:

Step 1. Heat the oil in a pan, add the bay leaves, cloves, cinnamon sticks and cardamoms and sauté over medium heat until they begin to crackle.

2. Add the diced onions and sauté until soft.

3. Add the ginger and garlic pastes, red chilli powder, and the ground lamb, stir and cook until the raw smell of the ingredients disappears.

4. Add the garam masala, crushed black pepper and yoghurt. Bring it to a slow boil, cover and simmer until the liquid evaporates.

5. Adjust the seasoning, salt and mace powder.

To Serve:

Serve garnished with fresh mint leaves, green coriander, fine ginger juliennes and slit green chilies and accompanied with a raita and rotis.

Nargisi Kofta

A rich minceball curry with the minceballs stuffed with boiled eggs. A party treat!

Serves: 4-5   Preparation time: 25 minutes   Cooking time: 30 minutes

Ingredients:

For the koftas:

Lamb, minced very finely	1 kg
Butter	50 gms/3^1/$_3$ tbs
Coriander powder	4 gms/^{3}/$_4$ tsp
Eggs	2
Eggs, boiled and chopped	4
Fennel powder (saunf)	4 gms/^{3}/$_4$ tsp
Garlic paste	25 gms/5 tsp
Ginger paste	25 gms/5 tsp
Green chillies, finely chopped	6 gms/2
Green coriander, finely chopped	10 gms/2 tsp
Onions, grated	20 gms/4 tsp
Raisins	50
Salt for seasoning	
White pepper powder	4 gms/^{3}/$_4$ tsp

For the gravy:

Bay leaves (tej patta)	2
Cinnamon sticks	3
Cloves	10 gms/2 tsp
Cream	10 ml/2 tsp
Garam masala	10 gms/2 tsp
Garlic paste	50 gms/3^1/$_3$ tbs
Ginger paste	50 gms/3^1/$_3$ tbs
Green cardamoms	10
Green coriander, chopped	15 gms/3 tsp
Mace powder (javitri)	4 gms/^{3}/$_4$ tsp
Oil	80 ml/5^1/$_3$ tbs
Onion paste	160 gms/^{3}/$_4$ cup
Red chilli powder	10 gms/2 tsp
Saffron strand, dissolved in 15 ml milk	1 gm/^{1}/$_5$ tsp

Salt for seasoning	
Tomatoes, skinned and chopped	350 gms/1^3/$_4$ cups
Vetivier (kewda)	3 drops

Lamb Mughlai

Method:

Step 1. Mix all the ingredients for the koftas, except the boiled eggs and raisins, with the lamb mince in a bowl. Mix thoroughly with a wooden spoon until the mixture sticks to the spoon. Season to taste with salt. Divide this mixture into 25 balls.

2. Stuff each meat ball with boiled egg and raisins and shape into a ball (kofta).

3. Heat the oil in a pan, add the bay leaves, cloves and cinnamon sticks, and sauté over medium heat for 30 seconds. Add the onion paste, ginger and garlic pastes, and sauté for 30 seconds. Add the red chilli powder, stir and cook for 3-4 minutes. Then add the chopped tomatoes, stir and cook.

4. Add the rest of the spices and simmer over medium heat until the oil separates from the tomato gravy.

5. Now add the koftas very carefully to the gravy. Add 1½ cups of hot water and cover and simmer for 10 minutes.

6. Add cream, the saffron mixture, mace powder and vetivier and remove from heat.

To Serve:

Serve with green coriander, accompanied by a vegetable preparation, raita and rotis or rice.

Lamb Mughlai

A most delicately flavoured lamb curry

Serves: 4-5   Preparation time: 15 minutes   Cooking time: 1 hour

Ingredients:

Lamb	1 kg	Ginger paste	50 gms/3$\frac{1}{3}$ tbs
Bay leaf (tej patta)	1	Green cardamoms	6
Black pepper	2 gms/½ tsp	Green chilli paste	50 gms/3$\frac{1}{3}$ tbs
Cashewnut paste	300 gms/1½ cups	Refined oil	200 gms/1 cup
Cinnamon sticks	4	Saffron	2 gms
Cloves	8	Salt to taste	
Egg, boiled	1	Yoghurt, whisked	100 gms/½ cup
Garlic paste	50 gms/3$\frac{1}{3}$ tbs		

Method:

Step 1. Heat the oil. Add the cinnamon, cardamoms, cloves and bay leaf and sauté over medium heat for 30 seconds.

2. Add the ginger, garlic and green chilli pastes. Cook thoroughly.

3. Add the yoghurt and lamb and cook on a low fire for 45 minutes.

4. When meat is tender, add the cashewnut paste, salt, pepper and saffron. Stir briefly and remove from heat.

To Serve:

Serve garnished with a boiled egg. Chicken mughlai can also be made using the same ingredients and method, substituting chicken for the lamb.

Safed Maas

Safed maas, literally 'white meat', is an ancient Rajasthani delicacy

Serves: 4-5   Preparation time: 15 minutes

Cooking time: 45 minutes

Ingredients:

Lamb, boneless	1½ kg
Almonds, blanched	60 gms/$\frac{1}{3}$ cup
Coconut pieces	50 gms/¼ cup
Cream	120 ml/$\frac{2}{3}$ cup
Ginger juliennes	20 gms/4 tsp
Green chillies, chopped	6
Lemon juice	10 ml/2 tsp
Oil	150 gms/¾ cup
Rose water (gulab jal)	5 ml/1 tsp
Salt to taste	
White cardamom powder	3 gms/$\frac{2}{3}$ tsp
White pepper powder	5 gms/1 tsp
Yoghurt, whisked	250 gms/1¼ cups

Method:

Step 1.   Clean and cut the lamb into 3 cm cubes. Place in a pan, add salt and water (1.5 litres) and boil for 5 minutes. Drain and wash the lamb.

2. Mix the yoghurt and white pepper well.

3. Put the almonds and coconut in a blender, add 60 ml water and blend for 4-5 minutes to a fine paste.

4. Heat the oil in a pan, add the blanched lamb, the spiced yoghurt, ginger, salt and water (800 ml/4 cups), cover and simmer, stirring occasionally, until the lamb is tender and the liquid has almost evaporated.

5. Add the almond and coconut paste and stir for 2 minutes. Sprinkle cardamom powder and stir.

6. Add cream, lemon juice and rose water and stir. Sprinkle chopped green chillies. Cover the pan, seal with dough and place on *dum* in a preheated oven (135 °C/270 °F) for 15 minutes.

To Serve:

Break the dough seal and transfer the cooked lamb to a shallow dish. Serve with rotis or steamed rice.

Paneer Dahi ke Kebab   48

Dum Alu Bhojpuri   60

Bharwan Shimla Mirch   56

Shahi Paneer   52

Palak Paneer   50

Vegetable Korma   63

Vegetables & Paneer

Tandoori Paneer Tikka

An ideal vegetarian appetizer

Serves: 4-5   Preparation time: 2¼ hours   Cooking time: 10 minutes

Ingredients:

Cottage cheese (paneer)	1 kg	Ginger paste	15 gms/3 tsp
Black cumin (shah jeera)	3 gms/²/₃ tsp	Gram flour (besan)/cornflour	30 gms/2 tbs
Butter to baste	50 gms/¼ cup	Lemon juice	25 ml/5 tsp
Chaat masala	10 gms/2 tsp	Red chilli powder	10 gms/2 tsp
Cottage cheese (paneer), grated	50 gms/¼ cup	Saffron	3 gms/²/₃ tsp
Cream	150 ml/¾ cup	Salt to taste	
Fenugreek (methi)	5 gms/1 tsp	Turmeric powder (haldi)	5 gms/1 tsp
Garam masala	10 gms/2 tsp	White pepper	5 gms/1 tsp
Garlic paste	15 gms/3 tsp	Yoghurt, hung	150 gms/¾ cup

Method:

Step 1. Wash and cut the paneer into small cubes (30 pieces).
2. Mix the black cumin, white pepper, garam masala, turmeric powder, two-thirds of the lemon juice and salt. Sprinkle over the paneer cubes. Keep aside for 1 hour in the refrigerator.
3. Mix cream, yoghurt and gram flour/cornflour in a bowl. Add the remaining ingredients, whisk well to make a fine batter.
4. Add the paneer cubes to this and marinate for at least 1 hour.
5. Preheat the oven to 150-75 ºC (300-50 ºF).
6. Thread the paneer cubes on a skewer, 2 cm apart.
7. Roast in an oven, tandoor or on a charcoal grill for 5-6 minutes. Baste with melted butter.

To Serve:

Sprinkle with chaat masala and the remaining lemon juice. Serve with a green salad and mint chutney.

Kastoori Paneer Tikka

Paneer flavoured with fenugreek

Serves: 4-5   Preparation time: 2¼ hours   Cooking time: 10 minutes

Ingredients:

Cottage cheese (paneer)	1 kg	Garlic paste	15 gms/3 tsp
Black cumin (shah jeera)	3 gms/²⁄₃ tsp	Ginger paste	15 gms/3 tsp
Butter to baste	50 gms/¼ cup	Gram flour (besan)/cornflour	30 gms/2 tbs
Chaat masala (optional)	10 gms/2 tsp	Lemon juice	25 ml/5 tsp
Cottage cheese (paneer), grated	50 gms/¼ cup	Red chilli powder	10 gms/2 tsp
Cream	100 ml/½ cup	Salt to taste	
Fenugreek, dried (methi)	20 gms/4 tsp	White pepper	5 gms/1 tsp
Garam masala	10 gms/2 tsp	Yoghurt, hung	150 gms/¾ cup

Method:

Step1. Wash and cut the paneer into 4 cm cubes (30 pieces).
    2. Mix the black cumin, white pepper, garam masala, two-thirds of the lemon juice and salt. Add the grated paneer to this mixture. Marinate for 1 hour in the refrigerator.
    3. Mix cream, yoghurt, gram flour/cornflour and dry fenugreek in a bowl. Add the remaining ingredients and whisk to a fine batter.
    4. Add the paneer cubes to this marinade and leave aside for at least 1 hour.
    5. Preheat the oven to 150-75 °C (300-50 °F).
    6. Thread the paneer cubes on a skewer, 2 cms apart.
    7. Roast in an oven, tandoor or on a charcoal grill for 5-6 minutes. Baste with melted butter.

To Serve:

Sprinkle with chaat masala and the remaining lemon juice. Serve with slices of cucumbers, tomatoes, onions and mint chutney.

Chutney Paneer Tikka

Paneer in mint chutney

Serves: 4-5   Preparation time: 2¼ hours   Cooking time: 10 minutes

Ingredients:

Cottage cheese (paneer)	1 kg	Ginger paste	15 gms/3 tsp
Black cumin (shah jeera)	3 gms/²⁄₃ tsp	Gram flour (besan)/cornflour	30 gms/2 tbs
Chaat masala (optional)	15 gms/3 tsp	Lemon juice	25 ml/5 tsp
Cottage cheese (paneer), grated	50 gms/¼ cup	Red chilli powder	10 gms/2 tsp
Cream	60 ml/¹⁄₃ cup	Salt to taste	
Fenugreek, dried (methi)	5 gms/1 tsp	White pepper	5 gms/1 tsp
Fresh mint chutney	250 gms/1¼ cups	Yoghurt,	
Garam masala	10 gms/2 tsp	hung	150 gms/¾ cup
Garlic paste	15 gms/3 tsp		

Method:

Step 1. Wash and cut the paneer into 4 cm cubes (30 pieces).
    2. Mix the black cumin, white pepper, garam masala, lemon juice and salt. Add the paneer to this mixture. Marinade for 1 hour in the refrigerator.
    3. Mix cream, yoghurt, gram flour/cornflour and fresh mint chutney. Add the remaining ingredients and whisk to a fine batter.
    4. Add the paneer cubes to this marinade and leave aside for at least 1 hour.

5. Preheat the oven to 150-75 °C (300-50 °F).
6. Thread the paneer cubes on a skewer, 2 cms apart.
7. Roast in an oven, tandoor or on a charcoal grill for 5-6 minutes. Baste with melted butter.

To Serve:

Sprinkle with chaat masala and lemon juice. Serve with slices of cucumbers, tomatoes, onions and mint chutney.

Kalyani Paneer Tikka

Stuffed, grilled paneer rolls

Serves: 4-5   Preparation time: 10 minutes   Cooking time: 20 minutes

Ingredients:

Cottage cheese (paneer), firm	500 gms	Potatoes, boiled and grated	100 gms/½ cup
		Raisins	100 gms/½ cup
For the stuffing:		Salt to taste	
Black cumin (shah jeera)	5 gms/1 tsp	Turmeric powder (haldi)	5 gms/1 tsp
Capsicum (green pepper), chopped	150 gms/¾ cup	White pepper powder	20 gms/4 tsp
Cayenne pepper (kashmiri red chilli)	10 gms/2 tsp		
Coconut powder	100 gms/½ cup	**For the coating:**	
Cottage cheese (paneer), grated	150 gms/¾ cup	Cornflour	100 gms/½ cup
Fenugreek (kastoori methi)	5 gms/1 tsp	Cream	100 ml/½ cup
Lemon juice	10 ml/2 tsp	Gram flour (besan)	50 gms/¼ cup
Mushrooms, chopped	150 gms/¾ cup	Green coriander, chopped	20 gms/4 tsp
Oil	75 ml/5 tbs	Saffron (a few strands)	0.5 gms
Onions, chopped	150 gms/¾ cup	Water	20 ml/4 tsp

Method:

Step 1. Slice the paneer lengthwise into pieces of 15 cm X 6 cm X 0.5 cm.
2. Heat the oil. Add mushrooms, capsicum, onion and coconut powder and sauté.
3. Add the grated paneer, potato and all the spices for the stuffing as well as the lemon juice.
4. Make a thick paste of gram flour and water for coating.
5. Smear the thick paste on one side of each paneer slice, and on the other side put 70-80 gms of the stuffing and make into a roll.
6. Mix the remaining ingredients for the coating.
7. Coat the stuffed paneer rolls with the coating and bake in a slow oven/tandoor for 10-12 minutes.

To Serve:

Sprinkle the tikkas with chaat masala and garnish with grated carrots and lemon wedges.

Kalyani Paneer Tikka

Tandoori Paneer Salad

A festive vegetarian starter

Serves: 4-5   Preparation time: 2 hours   Cooking time: 15 minutes

Ingredients:

Cottage cheese (paneer)	1 kg	Lemon juice	15 ml/1 tbs
Black cumin (shah jeera)	3 gms/$^2/_3$ tsp	Onions	20 gms/4 tsp
Butter for basting	50 gms/¼ cup	Pineapple cubes	20 gms/4 tsp
Capsicum (green pepper)	20 gms/4 tsp	Red chilli powder	10 gms/2 tsp
Chaat masala (optional)	10 gms/2 tsp	Saffron	3 gms/$^2/_3$ tsp
Cottage cheese (paneer), grated	50 gms/¼ cup	Salt to taste	
Cream	100 ml/½ cup	Tomatoes	20 gms/4 tsp
Garam masala	10 gms/2 tsp	Turmeric powder (haldi)	5 gms/1 tsp
Garlic paste	15 gms/3 tsp	White pepper powder	5 gms/1 tsp
Ginger paste	15 gms/3 tsp	Yoghurt, hung	150 gms/¾ cup
Gram flour/cornflour	30 gms/2 tbs		

Method:

Step 1. Wash and cut the paneer and vegetables into 4 cm cubes—paneer into 30 pieces and vegetables into 20 pieces each.

2. Mix black cumin, white pepper, garam masala, turmeric powder, two-thirds of the lemon juice and salt together. Marinate the paneer pieces in this mixture for 1 hour in the refrigerator.

3. Mix the cream, yoghurt, and gram flour/cornflour. Add all the remaining ingredients, except the butter, and whisk to a fine batter.

4. Add the paneer cubes, pineapple cubes and vegetables to the batter and marinate for at least 1 hour.

5. Preheat oven to 150-75 °C (300-50 °F).

6. Skewer 6 paneer cubes and 4 vegetables pieces per skewer (one portion) and pack tightly together.

7. Roast in an oven or tandoor or on a charcoal grill for 5-6 minutes. Baste with melted butter.

To Serve:

Sprinkle with chaat masala and the remaining lemon juice. Serve with slices of cucumbers, tomatoes, onions and mint chutney.

Paneer Dahi ke Kebab

Crispy sesame seed coated cottage cheese steak

Serves: 4-5   Preparation time: 30 minutes
Cooking time: 15 minutes

Ingredients:

Cottage cheese (paneer), finely grated	500 gms	Salt to taste	
Cardamom powder	2 gms/½ tsp	Sesame	
Egg (optional)	1	seeds	100 gms/½ cup
Garam masala	10 gms/2 tsp	White pepper	
Gram flour(besan)/cornflour	50 gms/¼ cup	powder	5 gms/1 tsp
Green chillies, chopped	5 gms/1 tsp	Yellow or red chilli	
Green coriander, chopped	10 gms/2 tsp	powder	6 gms/1$^1/_3$ tsp
Mace powder (javitri)	2 gms/½ tsp	Yoghurt,	
Oil	100 ml/½ cup	hung	400 gms/2 cups
Onions, finely chopped	100 gms/½ cup		

Method:

Step 1. Combine all the ingredients except the gram flour/cornflour, in a bowl. Mix with wooden spoon and season to taste. Add the gram flour/cornflour and mix for 2 minutes.

2. Divide the mixture into 20 equal portions. Make each portion into a round ball, roll it in your palm and press slightly to get a 4 cm patty. Cool the patties in the refrigerator for 20 minutes.
3. Heat the oil in a deep pan or a *kadhai*/wok. Shallow fry in a nonstick pan until golden crisp. Alternatively, you could lightly coat each patty with egg white, sprinkle with sesame seeds and shallow fry in a nonstick pan.

To Serve:

Serve with cucumber slices, tomato slices, onion slices and fresh mint chutney.

Paneer Seekh Kebab

Vegetarian skewered kebabs

Serves: 4-5   Preparation time: 15 minutes   Cooking time: 15 minutes

Ingredients:

Cottage cheese (paneer), grated fine	1 kg	Lemon juice	15 ml/1 tbs
Butter for basting	20 gms/4 tsp	Onions, grated	150 gms/¾ cup
Cornflour	15 gms/3 tsp	Red chilli powder	5 gms/1 tsp
Garam masala	10 gms/2 tsp	Salt for seasoning	
Ginger paste	25 gms/5 tsp	White pepper powder	5 gms/1 tsp
Green chillies, chopped	6		

Method:

Step 1. Mix all the ingredients, keeping the cornflour till the end.
2. Divide this mixture into 15 equal balls.
3. Preheat the oven to 150-75ºC (300-50 ºF).
4. Thread each ball through a skewer. Spread the balls by pressing them with a moistened palm along the length of the skewers into a finger-sized kebab, 8-10 cm long and 1 cm apart.
5. Roast in an oven or tandoor or on a charcoal grill for 5-6 minutes and baste with melted butter.

To Serve:

Remove from the skewers and serve with slices of cucumbers, tomatoes, onions and mint chutney.

NOTE: The paneer could be rolled into 8 cm-long fingers and sautéed in a frying pan with a little butter.

Paneer Seekh Kebab

Palak Paneer

A classic north Indian recipe

Serves: 4-5   Preparation time: 25 minutes   Cooking time: 30 minutes

Ingredients:

Spinach (palak) leaves	1 kg	Maize flour (makke ka atta)	20 gms/4 tsp
Cottage cheese (paneer) cubes	250 gms/1¼ cups	Onions, chopped	25 gms/5 tsp
Cream	10 gms/2 tsp	Red chilli powder	5 gms/1 tsp
Ghee (clarified butter)	30 gms/2 tbs	Salt to taste	
Ginger, cut fine	25 gms/5 tsp	Tomatoes, finely cut	10 gms/2 tsp
Green chillies, chopped	3	Water	2 litres/10 cups

Method:

Step 1. Remove the stalks of the spinach leaves. Wash very well and cut fine. Add water and salt and cook for 10 minutes. Drain the excess water and purée in a blender.

2. Add the paneer cubes to the purée and mix well. Add maize flour slowly and cook for 10 minutes. (This acts as a thickening agent.)

3. In a separate pan, heat the ghee. Brown the onions and most of the ginger. Add red chilli powder and stir. Pour this sauce over the paneer-spinach mixture. Stir well and cook through for 5 minutes.

To Serve:

Garnish with the remaining pieces of ginger, tomato pieces, green chillies and cream. Serve with a green salad and naan.

Methi Chaman

Exotic blend of fenugreek purée and cottage cheese cubes

Serves: 4-5   Preparation time: 10 minutes

Cooking time: 1 hour

Ingredients:

Fresh fenugreek (methi)	150 gms/¾ cup
or	
Dry fenugreek leaves	100 gms/½ cup
Spinach (palak)	450 gms/2¼ cups
Butter	30 gms/2 tbs
Cottage cheese (paneer), small cubes	500 gms
Garam masala	8 gms/1²/₃ tsp
Garlic, chopped (optional)	10 gms/2 tsp
Ginger juliennes	5 gms/1 tsp
Ginger paste	50 gms/3¹/₃ tbs
Green chilli paste	15 gms/3 tsp
Oil	30 ml/2 tbs
Onions, grated	50 gms/3¹/₃ tbs
Red chilli powder	5 gms/1 tsp
Salt to taste	
White pepper powder	5 gms/1 tsp

Method:

Step 1. Wash the fenugreek and spinach in running water and chop the leaves coarsely. Blanch in boiling salt water for 1 minute. Remove immediately and place in a bowl of cold water. Squeeze the water out of the leaves completely and grind in a food processor to a fine purée.

2. Heat the oil and butter in a *kadhai*/wok. Add the onions, ginger, green chilli paste and chopped garlic and sauté over low heat for 5-6 minutes. Add pepper, salt and red chillies.
3. Add the fenugreek and spinach purée and cook for 35-40 minutes over medium heat until the oil separates from the greens. Stir the mixture from time to time to avoid burning.
4. Add the paneer and sprinkle garam masala. Cover and cook for 10 minutes.

To Serve:

Sprinkle with ginger juliennes before serving.

Kadhai Paneer

Cubes of cottage cheese cooked in a kadhai. A chilli hot, semi-dry and colourful curry!

Serves: 4-5   Preparation time: 15 minutes   Cooking time: 10 minutes

Ingredients:

Cottage cheese (paneer)	600 gms	Ginger juliennes	15 gms/3 tsp
Black pepper	8 gms/1²/₃ tsp	Green coriander leaves, chopped	15 gms/3 tsp
Capsicum (green pepper)	40 gms/2²/₃ tbs	Onions, chopped	40 gms/¼ cup
Coriander powder	10 gms/2 tsp	Red chillies, whole	15
Coriander seeds	10 gms/2 tsp	Refined oil	40 gms/2²/₃ tbs
Fenugreek powder (methi)	5 gms/1 tsp	Salt to taste	
Garam masala	8 gms/1²/₃ tsp	Tomato purée	150 ml/¾ cup

Method:

Step 1. Cut the paneer into fingers. Cut the capsicum into halves, deseed and make juliennes or cut into small, even squares.
2. Pound the red chillies and coriander seeds with a pestle to a powder.

3. Heat the oil in a *kadhai*/wok and sauté the onions and capsicum over medium heat for 2 minutes.
4. Add the pounded spices and two-thirds of the chopped ginger and stir for 1 minute. Add the tomato purée and salt, bring to a boil and simmer until the oil separates from the gravy.
5. Add the paneer and stir gently for 2-3 minutes.
6. Sprinkle with fenugreek powder, garam masala powder, ground coriander and black pepper. Stir.

To Serve:

Garnish with green coriander leaves and the remaining ginger juliennes. Serve with roti or parantha and salad or raita.

Kadhai Paneer

Shahi Paneer

Cottage cheese curried in yoghurt with cashewnuts

Serves: 4-5   Preparation time: 30 minutes   Cooking time: 20 minutes

Ingredients:

Cottage cheese (paneer), small cubes	1kg	Green cardamoms	6
Bay leaves (tej patta)	2	Mace powder (javitri)	3 gms/^{2}/$_3$ tsp
Cardamom powder	3 gms/^{2}/$_3$ tsp	Oil	80 ml/5^1/$_3$ tbs
Cashewnut paste	10 gms/2 tsp	Onions, quartered, boiled and ground	200 gms/1 cup
Cinnamon sticks	3	Red chilli powder	10 gms/2 tsp
Cloves	6	Saffron (dissolved in 15 ml milk)	0.5 gm
Coriander powder	5 gms/1 tsp	Salt to taste	
Double cream	120 ml/^{2}/$_3$ cup	Turmeric powder (haldi)	4 gms/¾ tsp
Garam masala	8 gms/1^2/$_3$ tsp	Vetivier (kewda)	3 drops
Garlic paste	40 gms/2^2/$_3$ tbs	Yoghurt, made from cream, whisked	180 gms/¾ cup
Ginger paste	40 gms/2^2/$_3$ tbs		

Method:

Step 1. Heat the oil in a pan, add the cloves, bay leaves, cinnamon stick and green cardamoms sauté over medium heat until they begin to crackle. Add the onion paste and sauté for 2-3 minutes.

2. Add the ginger and garlic pastes, red chilli, turmeric powder, coriander powder, cashewnut paste and salt.

3. Add the paneer cubes, stir and cook for further 5 minutes.

4. Add the whisked yoghurt and half a cup of warm water, bring it to a slow boil and then simmer until the oil separates from the gravy.

5. Reduce heat and add the cream, garam masala, cardamom powder, mace powder, vetivier and saffron mixture.

To Serve:

Serve with any dry vegetable preparation and rotis.

Zafrani Kofta Curry

An exotic curry made with cottage cheese, eggs and saffron

Serves: 4-5   Preparation time: 15 minutes   Cooking time: 45 minutes

Ingredients:

Cottage cheese (paneer), grated	500 gms	Green coriander, chopped	5 gms/1 tsp
Cashewnut pieces	50 gms/¼ cup	Onions, chopped	100 gms/½ cup
Coriander powder	25 gms/5 tsp	Red chilli powder	4 gms/¾ tsp
Eggs	2	Saffron (dissolved in 1 tbs milk)	1 gm
Fenugreek powder (methi)	2 gms/½ tsp	Salt to taste	
Garam masala	3 gms/^{2}/$_3$ tsp	Turmeric powder (haldi)	3 gms/^{2}/$_3$ tsp
Garlic paste	25 gms/5 tsp	White pepper powder	2 gms/½ tsp
Ghee	100 gms/½ cup	Yoghurt	100 gms/½ cup
Ginger paste	25 gms/5 tsp		

Method:

Step 1. To the grated paneer add the white pepper, cashewnut pieces, eggs and salt to taste.

2. Divide into 16 equal portions and make into balls.

3. Heat the ghee. Deep fry the balls in hot ghee until golden. Remove from the pan.

4. In the remaining ghee add the chopped onions, garlic, ginger pastes, red chilli powder, coriander powder and turmeric powder. Cook for 10 minutes till the mixture turns brown and separates from the ghee.

5. Add garam masala, half the fenugreek powder and yoghurt and cook for about 10 minutes.

6. Add the koftas very slowly to the gravy and simmer for 5 minutes.

To Serve:

Sprinkle the remaining fenugreek powder, saffron dissolved in a tablespoon of milk and chopped green coriander. Serve with naan or roti.

Paneer Birbali

Cottage cheese curried in tomatoes and garnished with cream

Serves: 4-5   Preparation time: 10 minutes   Cooking time: 20 minutes

Ingredients:

Cottage cheese (paneer), block	1 kg	Ginger paste	40 gms/2²/₃ tbs
Bay leaves (tej patta)	2	Green cardamoms	3 gms/²/₃ tsp
Cashewnuts	100 gms/½ cup	Green coriander, chopped	15 gms/3 tsp
Cinnamon sticks	3	Mace powder (javitri)	3 gms/²/₃ tsp
Cream	6 gms/1¹/₃ tsp	Milk	50 ml/3¹/₃ tbs
Cumin seeds	3 gms/²/₃ tsp	Oil	200 ml/1 cup
Garlic paste	40 gms/2²/₃ tbs	Onions, chopped	100 gms/½ cup
Ginger juliennes	6 gms/1¹/₃ tsp	Red chilli powder	10 gms/2 tsp
Gram flour (besan) or		Salt to taste	
maize flour (makke ka atta)	150 gms/¾ cup	Tomatoes, chopped	300 gms/1½ cups

Method:

Step 1. Heat 80 ml (¹/₃ cup) oil in a heavy pan. Add cardamoms, bay leaves, cumin seeds and cinnamon sticks and sauté over medium heat for 30 seconds.

2. Add the ginger and garlic pastes, red chilli powder and onions and sauté for 5 minutes. Add the tomatoes and 1½ cups of water, cover and cook over medium heat for 5-10 minutes. Uncover, stir and cook for another 5 minutes or until oil separates from the gravy.

3. Add mace, salt and three-fourths of the cream. Strain the gravy and keep aside.

4. Mix the gram flour in the milk to make a thick batter. Beat the batter for 3 minutes. Coat the paneer block with the batter. Heat the remaining oil in a pan and shallow fry the block until light brown.

5. Slice the paneer block lengthwise into 4 cm cubes, place on a platter and pour the hot sauce over it.

To Serve:

Garnish with chopped coriander leaves and ginger juliennes. Sprinkle with crushed cashewnuts.

Achari Paneer

A pickled preserve

Serves: 4-5   Preparation time: 15 minutes   Cooking time: 15 minutes

Ingredients:

Cottage cheese (paneer), cubed	1 kg	Lemon juice	20 ml/4 tsp
Asafoetida (heeng)	0.5 gms	Mustard seeds (raee)	7 gms/1½ tsp
Black cumin seed (shah jeera)	5 gms/1 tsp	Olive/mustard oil	110 ml/½ cup
Black pepper, crushed	6 gms/1¹/₃ tsp	Onions, chopped fine	200 gms/1 cup
Cloves	10	Red chilli powder	10 gms/2 tsp
Fenugreek seeds (methi)	8 gms/1²/₃ tsp	Red chillies, whole	16
Garlic, whole cloves	6	Salt to taste	
Garlic paste	60 gms/4 tbs	Sugar	10 gms/2 tsp
Ginger paste	60 gms/4 tbs	Turmeric powder (haldi)	10 gms/2 tsp
Green cardamoms	10	Yoghurt, whisked	300 gms/1½ cups
Green coriander, chopped	10 gms/2 tsp		

Method:

Step 1. Heat the oil in a pan to smoking point. Add the cloves, cardamoms, mustard seeds, fenugreek seeds, whole red chillies and cumin seeds and stir.

2. Add the chopped onions. Reduce the heat immediately and sauté over medium heat until onions are brown.

3. Add the ginger and garlic pastes, red chilli powder, turmeric powder and asafoetida, stir and cook for 3-4 minutes. Add the yoghurt, bring it to a boil and simmer over low heat until the oil separates from the gravy.

4. Add the paneer cubes, salt, pepper, sugar, garlic cloves and lemon juice, stir and cook for 1 minute.

To Serve:

Transfer into a serving dish and garnish with green coriander.

NOTE: This dish could be kept in a sterilized bottle in the refrigerator for 5-7 days without the green coriander.

Paneer Capsicum Bhujia

Cottage cheese delicately flavoured with capsicum

Serves: 4-5   Preparation time: 15 minutes   Cooking time: 15 minutes

Ingredients:

Cottage cheese (paneer), small cubes	600 gms	Oil	60 ml/4 tbs
Capsicum (green pepper)	150 gms/¾ cup	Onions	150 gms/¾ cup
Cumin seeds (jeera)	3 gms/²/₃ tsp	Red chilli powder	5 gms/1 tsp
Garam masala	15 gms/3 tsp	Salt for seasoning	
Green cardamoms	3	Tomatoes	150 gms/¾ cup
Green coriander, chopped	15 gms/3 tsp	Turmeric powder (haldi)	8 gms/1²/₃ tsp
Lemon juice	10 ml/2 tsp		

Method:

Step 1. Dice the capsicum, tomatoes and onions into small pieces.
2. Heat the oil in a pan. Add the cardamoms and cumin seeds and sauté over medium heat until they begin to crackle.
3. Add the turmeric powder and red chilli powder and sauté for 30 seconds.
4. Add the capsicum, onions and tomatoes and sauté for another 30 seconds over high heat.
5. Add paneer pieces, garam masala and salt. Sauté for 30 seconds, cover and cook for 6 minutes.

To Serve:

Sprinkle with green coriander and lemon juice before serving.

Paneer Jalfrezi

Dry cottage cheese curry with vinegar

Serves: 4-5   Preparation time: 15 minutes   Cooking time: 15 minutes

Ingredients:

Cottage cheese (paneer), cubed (2 cm)	600 gms	Lemon juice	10 ml/2 tsp
Bay leaves (tej patta)	2	Oil	60 ml/4 tbs
Capsicum (green pepper)	150 gms/¾ cup	Onions	150 gms/¾ cup
Cumin seeds (jeera)	3 gms/²/₃ tsp	Red chilli powder	15 gms/3 tsp
Garam masala	15 gms/3 tsp	Salt to taste	
Ginger juliennes	5 gms/1 tsp	Tomatoes	150 gms/¾ cup
Green cardamoms	3	Turmeric powder (haldi)	8 gms/1²/₃ tsp
Green coriander, chopped	15 gms/3 tsp	Vinegar, white or malt	30 ml/2 tbs

Method:

Step 1. Cut the capsicum, onions and tomatoes into 2 cm squares.
2. Heat the oil in a pan, add the green cardamoms, bay leaves and cumin seeds and sauté over medium heat until they begin to crackle.
3. Add the turmeric powder and red chilli powder and sauté for 30 seconds.

4. Add the capsicum, onions and tomatoes and sauté for another 30 seconds over high heat.
5. Add the paneer, vinegar, garam masala and salt. Sauté for 30 seconds, cover and cook for 6 minutes.

To Serve:

Garnish with ginger juliennes, green coriander and sprinkle lemon juice before serving.

Paneer Capsicum Bhujia

To Serve:

Sprinkle with green coriander, lemon juice and serve hot with naan or roti.

Paneer Do Piaza

Cottage cheese with double the onions!

Serves: 4-5   Preparation time: 10 minutes
Cooking time: 10 minutes

Ingredients:

Cottage cheese (paneer), cut into cubes	900 gms
Button onions	300 gms/1½ cups
Capsicum (green pepper), cut into squares	150 gms/¾ cup
Cumin seeds (jeera)	3 gms/⅔ tsp
Garam masala	15 gms/3 tsp
Green cardamoms	3
Green coriander, chopped	15 gms/3 tsp
Lemon juice	10 ml/2 tsp
Oil	60 ml/4 tbs
Red chilli powder	5 gms/1 tsp
Salt to taste	
Tomatoes, cut into cubes	150 gms/¾ cup
Turmeric powder (haldi)	8 gms/1⅔ tsp

Method:

Step 1. Heat the oil in a pan. Add cardamoms and cumin seed and sauté over medium heat until they begins to crackle. Add the turmeric and red chilli powder and sauté for 30 seconds.

2. Add the capsicum, button onions and tomatoes and sauté for another 30 seconds over high heat.

3. Add the paneer, garam masala and salt and sauté for 30 seconds.

4. Cover and cook for 6 minutes.

Bharwan Shimla Mirch

Capsicum stuffed with a spiced potato filling

Serves: 4-5   Preparation time: 15 minutes   Cooking time: 1 hour

Ingredients:

Capsicums (green pepper), each approximately 70 gms	10	Salt to taste	
		White pepper	5 gms/1 tsp
Butter for basting	40 gms/2²/₃ tbs	**For the sauce:**	
Cashewnuts, chopped	20 gms/4 tsp	Bay leaf (tej patta)	1
Garam masala	8 gms/1²/₃ tsp	Cream	60 ml/4 tbs
Ginger, finely chopped	10 gms/2 tsp	Garlic cloves	10 gms/3
Green chillies, finely chopped	10 gms/2 tsp	Green cardamoms	3 gms/²/₃ tsp
Green coriander, chopped	15 gms/3 tsp	Mace powder (javitri)	3 gms/²/₃ tsp
Oil	60 ml/4 tbs	Oil	25 ml/5 tsp
Onions, chopped	100 gms/½ cup	Onions, sliced	20 gms/¼ cup
Potatoes, boiled and mashed	750 gms	Salt to taste	
Raisins	20 gms/4 tsp	Tomatoes	300 gms/1½ cups

Method:

Step 1. Heat the oil in a pan and sauté the onions, cashewnuts and raisins over medium heat for 5-6 minutes.

2. Add the white pepper, garam masala, green chillies, finely chopped ginger, half of the green coriander and salt. Add the potatoes and stir for 5 minutes. Remove from the heat.

3. Fill each capsicum with the potato mixture and arrange the capsicums in a greased baking dish. Bake at 175 °C (350 °F) for 25-30 minutes. Baste with melted butter.

4. To make the sauce, heat the oil in a pan, sauté the cardamoms, bay leaf, onions, garlic cloves and tomatoes. Add 2 cups of water and cook for 30 minutes. Strain sauce through a fine sieve. Add the mace, salt and cream and stir.

To Serve:

Remove the capsicums from the oven and arrange them on a platter. Pour the sauce over the capsicums, sprinkle with the remaining half of the green coriander and serve.

Subz Jalfrezi

A vegetarian delicacy. Hot pepper corn, lemon curry

Serves: 4-5   Preparation time: 10 minutes   Cooking time: 15 minutes

Ingredients:

Button mushrooms	150 gms/¾ cup	Green coriander, chopped	15 gms/3 tsp
Button onions	150 gms/¾ cup	Oil	80 ml/5¹/₃ tbs
Capsicum (green pepper)	150 gms/¾ cup	Onions, chopped	100 gms/½ cup
Carrots	150 gms/¾ cup	Red chilli powder	10 gms/2 tsp
Cauliflower, cut into small flowerettes	150 gms/¾ cup	Red chillies, whole	5
Potatoes	150 gms/¾ cup	Salt to taste	
Cumin powder (jeera)	3 gms/²/₃ tsp	Sugar	5 gms/1 tsp
Garam masala	15 gms/3 tsp	Tomatoes, chopped	150 gms/¾ cup
Ginger juliennes	20 gms/4 tsp	Turmeric powder (haldi)	8 gms/1²/₃ tsp
Green cardamoms	5	Vinegar, white	30 ml/2 tbs
Green chillies, slit	15 gms/3 tsp	White pepper powder	5 gms/1 tsp

Method:

Step 1. Heat the oil in a pan, add green cardamoms and whole red chillies and sauté over medium heat until they begin to crackle. Add chopped onions and sauté until light brown. Add the turmeric powder, red chilli powder, white pepper and cumin powder and sauté for 30 seconds.

2. Cut the capsicum into long strips and add them to potatoes, carrots, button onions, cauliflower, tomatoes and button mushrooms and sauté for another 30 seconds over high heat.

3. Add the sugar, vinegar and garam masala and sauté for 30 seconds. Cover and cook for 6 minutes.

To Serve:

Season with salt and garnish with green chillies, ginger julienne and green coriander.

Hyderabadi Mirchi ka Salan

For the real hot curry eaters, a curry to set you on fire

Serves: 4-5   Preparation time: 15 minutes   Cooking time: 35 minutes

Ingredients:

Green chillies, large	200 gms/1 cup	Salt to taste	
Coconut, desiccated	50 gms/¼ cup	Sesame seeds (til)	50 gms/3²/₃ tbs
Coriander seeds, roasted	20 gms/4 tsp	Tamarind (imli)	60 gms/3 lemon sized balls
Cumin powder (jeera)	20 gms/4 tsp	Turmeric powder (haldi)	5 gms/1 tsp
Garlic paste	15 gms/3 tsp		
Ginger paste	15 gms/3 tsp	**For tempering:**	
Oil	500 ml/2½ cups	Cumin seeds (jeera)	3 gms/²/₃ tsp
Onions, sliced	1 kg	Curry leaves	20
Peanuts	50 gms/¼ cup	Mustard seed	3 gms/²/₃ tsp
Red chilli powder	12 gms/2½ tsp	Onion seed (kalonji)	3 gms/²/₃ tsp

Method:

Step 1. Soak tamarind in warm water for 10 minutes and squeeze out the pulp.
2. Broil the coconut, peanuts and sesame seeds in a frying pan. Grind to a fine paste. Add the coriander seeds, cumin powder, red chilli powder, turmeric, ginger and garlic pastes and a little salt to this ground pastes and mix thoroughly.
3. Fry the sliced onions in oil till golden brown. Drain from the oil and grind into a paste.
4. Mix the two pastes together.
5. Slit and deseed the green chillies and stuff with the ground paste. Fry the green chillies till they are golden brown.
6. Heat the remaining oil and sauté the mustard seed, onion seed, curry leaves and cumin. Add any left over ground paste and the tamarind pulp and cook on a slow fire for 10 minutes.

To Serve:

Add the fried green chillies and simmer for another 10 minutes and serve.

Mattar Paneer

A dry curry of peas and cottage cheese

Serves: 4-5   Preparation time: 15 minutes   Cooking time: 30 minutes

Ingredients:

Cottage cheese (paneer), cut into 1 cm cubes	250 gms/1¼ cups	Ginger paste	30 gms/6 tsp
Green peas, fresh or frozen	400 gms/2 cups	Green cardamom powder	3 gms/²/₃ tsp
Black cumin (shah jeera)	3 gms/²/₃ tsp	Green cardamoms	6
Cashewnut paste	100 gms/½ cup	Green chilli paste	25 gms/5 tsp
Cinnamon sticks	2	Green coriander, chopped	15 gms/3 tsp
Cloves	6	Oil	60 ml/4 tbs
Cream	80 ml/5¹/₃ tbs	Onions, grated	120 gms/²/₃ cup
Garam masala	10 gms/2 tsp	Salt to taste	
Garlic paste	30 gms/6 tsp	White pepper powder	3 gms/²/₃ tsp
Ginger juliennes	5 gms/1 tsp	Yoghurt, whisked	200 gms/1 cup

Method:

Step 1. Heat the oil in a saucepan and lightly sauté the paneer cubes, a few at a time, till golden. Keep aside.
2. To the left over oil add the black cumin, green cardamoms, cloves and cinnamon and sauté till they begin to crackle. Add the grated onion, ginger, garlic and green chilli pastes, pepper, salt and garam masala and sauté for 4-5 minutes.
3. Add the cashewnut paste and yoghurt and cook for 5-6 minutes. Add the green peas and cook over a low fire, stirring occasionally, until the gravy separates from the oil.
4. Add the fried paneer cubes and cream and simmer for a few minutes.

To Serve:

Transfer to a bowl and garnish with green coriander and ginger juliennes and sprinkle with green cardamom powder (The paneer can be substituted with 250 gms of mushroom, which do not need to be previously fried.)

Alu ki Tarkari

Spiced potato creole

Serves: 4-5   Preparation time: 10 minutes   Cooking time: 30 minutes

Ingredients:

Potatoes, boiled and cubed	900 gms/4½ cups	Oil	80 ml/5⅓ tbs
Butter	20 gms/4 tsp	Onions, chopped	100 gms/½ cup
Coriander powder	8 gms/1⅔ tsp	Red chilli powder	10 gms/2 tsp
Garlic, chopped	20 gms/4 tsp	Red chillies, whole, cut into half	5
Ginger, chopped	20 gms/4 tsp	Salt for seasoning	
Green chillies, chopped	10 gms/2 tsp	Tomatoes, skinned and chopped	300 gms/1½ cups
Lemon juice	15 ml/1 tbs	Turmeric powder (haldi)	5 gms/1 tsp
Mustard seeds	5 gms/1 tsp		

Method:

Step 1. Heat the oil in a pan. Sauté the whole red chillies and mustard seeds over medium heat until they begin to crackle.
   2. Add the chopped onions, garlic, ginger and saute over high heat for 5-6 minutes.
      Add the red chilli powder, turmeric powder, coriander powder and salt and stir.
   3. Add the chopped tomatoes and simmer on low heat until the oil separates from the gravy.
   4. Add the boiled potato cubes, chopped green chillies, lemon juice and salt, stir and cook for 5 minutes.

To Serve:

Melt the butter and pour over the potatoes before serving. Garnish with green coriander.

Alu Palak

Ginger flavoured potatoes in spinach cream

Serves: 4-5   Preparation time: 25 minutes   Cooking time: 25 minutes

Ingredients:

Potatoes, boiled	250 gms/1¼ cups	Onions, chopped	25 gms/5 tsp
Spinach (palak)	1 kg	Red chilli powder or	5 gms/1 tsp
Cream	10 gms/2 tsp	Green chillies, chopped	3
Ghee (clarified butter)	30 gms/2 tbs	Salt to taste	
Ginger, chopped fine	25 gms/5 tsp	Water	2 litres/10 cups
Maize flour (makke ka atta)	10 gms/2 tsp		

Method:

Step 1. Remove the stalks of the spinach leaves. Wash the leaves well and chop fine. Add water and salt and cook for 10 minutes. Drain the water away and purée the spinach.
   2. Add the potato cubes to the purée and mix well.
   3. Add maize flour slowly and cook for 10 minutes. (This acts as a thickening agent.)
   4. In a separate pan, heat the ghee and brown the onions and half the ginger. Add the red chilli powder or green chillies and sauté for a 60 seconds.
   5. Pour this over the potato-spinach mixture, stir well and heat through.

To Serve:

Serve garnished with ginger juliennes and cream, accompanied by a dal, green salad and roti.

Alu Methi

Golden fried potatoes in spinach fenugreek purée

Serves: 4-5   Preparation time: 10 minutes   Cooking time: 40 minutes

Ingredients:

Fresh fenugreek (methi) or	150 gms/¾ cup	Ginger, chopped very fine	50 gms/3⅓ tbs
Dry fenugreek leaves (methi)	100 gms/½ cup	Green chilli, paste	15 gms/3 tsp
Potatoes, boiled and golden fried		Oil	30 ml/2 tbs
(button or cut into cubes)	500 gms/2½ cups	Onions, grated	50 gms/¼ cup
Spinach (palak)	450 gms/2¼ cups	Red chilli powder	5 gms/1 tsp
Butter	30 gms/2 tbs	Salt to taste	
Garam masala	8 gms/1⅔ tsp	White pepper powder	5 gms/1 tsp
Garlic, chopped fine (optional)	10 gms/2 tsp		

Method:

Step 1. Wash the fenugreek and spinach and shred the leaves. Blanch the shredded leaves in boiling salt water for a minute. Remove immediately and place under cold water. Drain water completely and blend the leaves to a fine purée.

2. Heat the oil and butter in a pan, add the grated onions, two-thirds of the ginger, the green chilli paste and chopped garlic and saute over low heat for 5-6 minutes. Add the pepper, garam masala, salt and red chilli powder and stir.

3. Add the fenugreek-spinach purée and cook for 15 minutes over medium heat until the oil separates from the mixture.

4. Add the boiled and golden fried potatoes and cook for another 10 minutes.

To Serve:

Sprinkle with chopped ginger before serving.

The ever popular potato in different preparations

Dum Alu Bhojpuri

Stuffed potatoes—Bhojpuri style

Serves: 4-5   Preparation time: 20 minutes   Cooking time: 20 minutes

Ingredients:

Potatoes, small round (20-25 pcs)	600 gms	Ghee (clarified butter)	15 gms/1 tbs
Potatoes (boiled and grated)	200 gms	Ginger paste	30 gms/2 tbs
		Green cardamoms	6
For the gravy:		Lemon juice	15 ml/1 tbs
Bay leaf (tej patta)	1	Onions, grated	80 gms/$5\frac{1}{3}$ tbs
Black cumin seeds (shah jeera)	3 gms/$\frac{2}{3}$ tsp	Red chilli powder	10 gms/2 tsp
Cloves	6	Refined oil	50 ml/$3\frac{1}{3}$ tbs
Garam masala or	10 gms/2 tsp	Salt to taste	
Cinnamon sticks	2	Turmeric powder (haldi)	5 gms/1 tsp
Garlic paste	30 gms/2 tbs	Yoghurt, whisked	150 gms/$\frac{3}{4}$ cup

Method:

Step 1. Heat the ghee in a pan and add the grated onions, ginger and garlic pastes and fry for 4-5 minutes. Add potatoes, red chilli powder, turmeric powder and garam masala. Season with lemon juice and salt. Keep aside.

2. Boil and peel the small potatoes. Scoop and hollow them.
3. Fry these potatoes carefully and stuff each potato with the potato mixture of Step 1. Keep aside covered.
4. Heat the refined oil in a pan over medium heat. Add bay leaf, cinnamon sticks, cloves, green cardamoms, black cumin seed and fry for 30-50 seconds or until they begin to crackle.
5. Add the remaining grated onions, ginger and garlic pastes and fry for 2-3 minutes.
6. Add turmeric powder and red chilli powder and fry over medium heat for 5-6 minutes.
7. Add whisked yoghurt. Stir and cook till moisture evaporates. Add garam masala. Season to taste with salt.
8. Arrange the stuffed potatoes carefully inside the pan. Sprinkle the remaining garam masala and lemon juice.
9. Cover the lid and cook for 3-4 minutes on very low heat.

To Serve:

Transfer to a serving platter and garnish with chopped coriander, ginger juliennes and lace with fresh cream. Serve with rice or pooris.

Alu Gobi Sukhi

Peppy potatoes and spicy cauliflower

Serves: 4-5   Preparation time: 10 minutes   Cooking time: 40 minutes

Ingredients:

Cauliflower, cut into small pieces	500 gms	Green cardamoms	5
Potatoes, medium, cut into quarters	500 gms	Green coriander, chopped	15 gms/1 tbs
Bay leaves (tej patta)	2	Oil	80 ml/$\frac{1}{3}$ cup
Black pepper, crushed	5	Onions, sliced and chopped	100 gms/$\frac{1}{2}$ cup
Coriander powder	10 gms/2 tsp	Red chilli powder	8 gms/$1\frac{2}{3}$ tsp
Cumin seeds (jeera)	6 gms/$1\frac{1}{3}$ tsp	Red chillies, whole, cut into half	5
Garam masala	15 gms/3 tsp	Salt for seasoning	
Garlic paste	40 gms/$2\frac{2}{3}$ tbs	Tomatoes, sliced and chopped	200 gms/1 cup
Ginger juliennes	10 gms/2 tsp	Turmeric powder (haldi)	5 gms/1 tsp
Ginger paste	40 gms/$2\frac{2}{3}$ tbs		

Method:

Step 1. Heat the oil in a pan. Add the bay leaves, cardamoms, whole red chillies and cumin seeds. Sauté over medium heat.

2. Add the chopped onions, ginger, garlic pastes, turmeric powder, red chilli powder and coriander powder and sauté for 45-60 seconds. Add tomatoes and cook for another 5 minutes.
3. Add the cauliflower and potatoes and cook over medium heat for 10 minutes. Add 200 ml (1 cup) of water, cover and cook for 10 minutes on low heat. Season with salt, black pepper and garam masala and stir.

To Serve:

Serve garnished with the green coriander and ginger juliennes.

Gobi Adrekhi

Cauliflower seasoned with ginger

Serves: 4-5   Preparation time: 10 minutes   Cooking time: 25 minutes

Ingredients:

Cauliflower, cut into small pieces	1 kg	Oil	75 ml/^{1}/$_3$ cup
Butter	10 gms/2 tsp	Onions, finely chopped	150 gms/^{3}/$_4$ cup
Coriander powder	10 gms/2 tsp	Red chilli powder	10 gms/2 tsp
Garam masala	10 gms/2 tsp	Salt to taste	
Garlic paste	20 gms/4 tsp	Tomatoes, skinned and chopped	100 gms/^{1}/$_2$ cup
Ginger juliennes	10 gms/2 tsp	Turmeric powder (haldi)	10 gms/2 tsp
Ginger paste	20 gms/4 tsp	White pepper powder	5 gms/1 tsp
Green coriander, chopped	10 gms/2 tsp		

Method:

Step 1. Heat the oil in a pan. Add the onions and sauté over medium heat. Add the ginger and garlic pastes, turmeric powder, red chilli powder, white pepper, coriander powder and chopped tomatoes and sauté for 45-60 seconds.

2. Add the washed and drained cauliflower, stir and add 200 ml (1 cup) of water. Cover and cook for 15 minutes till the liquid dries up. Season with salt and garam masala.

3. Lightly sauté the ginger juliennes in butter.

To Serve:

Garnish the cauliflower with green coriander and ginger juliennes.

Gobi Musallam

Baked whole cauliflower with spiced yoghurt and cashewnuts

Serves: 4-5   Preparation time: 10 minutes   Cooking time: 45 minutes

Ingredients:

Cauliflower, 5 small whole ones	1 kg	Mace powder (javitri)	3 gms/^{2}/$_3$ tsp
Butter	30 gms/2 tbs	Oil	80 ml/^{1}/$_3$ cup
Cashewnuts or almonds, roasted	100 gms/^{1}/$_2$ cup	Oil for deep frying	500 gms/2^1/$_2$ cups
Garam masala	10 gms/2 tsp	Onions, chopped	200 gms/1 cup
Garlic paste	25 gms/5 tsp	Red chilli powder	10 gms/2 tsp
Ginger paste	25 gms/5 tsp	Salt to taste	
Green cardamoms	6	Turmeric powder (haldi)	5 gms/1 tsp
Lemon juice	15 ml/1 tbs	Yoghurt, whisked	200 gms/1 cup

Method:

Step 1. Heat the oil for frying. Deep fry each cauliflower over medium heat until almost cooked.

2. In the same oil, fry the onions and cashewnuts (saving a few for the garnish!) and then grind to a fine paste.

3. Heat 80 ml oil in a pan, add the cardamoms and sauté for a few second. Add the turmeric powder, red chilli powder, ginger and garlic pastes and garam masala and cook for 30 seconds.

4. Add the onions, cashewnut paste and whisked yoghurt and cook for 10 minutes on low heat. Season to taste with salt.

5. Arrange the fried cauliflower in a baking dish, and pour the gravy over each cauliflower. Bake in a moderate oven to 175 °C (350 °F) for 10 minutes.

To Serve:

Garnish with golden fried cashewnuts, dot with melted butter and sprinkle with lemon juice and mace powder before serving.

Gobi Gulistan

A crispy carom seeds-cauliflower kebab

Serves: 4-5   Preparation time: 15 minutes   Cooking time: 15 minutes

Ingredients:

Cauliflower, 5 small whole ones,	1 kg	Green coriander, finely chopped	20 gms/4 tsp
Carom seeds (ajwain)	6 gms/1⅓ tsp	Lemon juice	3 ml/⅔ tsp
Garam masala	8 gms/1⅔ tsp	Oil	500 ml/2½ cups
Garlic paste	10 gms/2 tsp	Red or yellow chilli powder	10 gms/2 tsp
Ginger paste	10 gms/2 tsp	Salt to taste	
Gram flour (besan)/white flour/		Turmeric powder (haldi)	10 gms/2 tsp
maize flour (makke ka atta)	200 gms/1 cup	Yoghurt	100 gms/½ cup
Green chillies, finely chopped	20 gms/4 tsp		

Method:

Step 1. Boil sufficient water to immerse the cauliflowers. Add salt and turmeric powder.
2. Gradually add the cauliflowers to this brine solution. Cook for 8-10 minutes over medium heat until the cauliflowers are half cooked. Drain and keep aside.
3. In a bowl make a batter with the gram flour (besan)/white flour, carom seeds, lemon juice, yoghurt, ginger, garlic pastes, garam masala, chilli powder and salt. The batter consistency should be thick and smooth.
4. Heat the oil in a *kadhai*/wok. Dip each cauliflower into the batter, coat evenly and deep fry over medium heat till golden.

To Serve:

Cut each cauliflower in four and serve on a platter, garnished with green coriander and green chillies. Serve with fresh cucumbers, sliced tomatoes and mint chutney.

Kadhai Mattar

A chilli hot and colourful dish

Serves: 4-5   Preparation time: 10 minutes   Cooking time: 15 minutes

Ingredients:

Green peas, fresh or frozen	900 gms
Black cardamom powder	5 gms/1 tsp
Black pepper powder	8 gms/1⅔ tsp
Coriander seeds, crushed	15 gms/3 tsp
Dry fenugreek leaves (methi)	25 gms/5 tsp
Garam masala	15 gms/3 tsp
Garlic paste	25 gms/5 tsp
Ginger paste	25 gms/5 tsp
Green coriander, chopped	15 gms/3 tsp
Green chillies, chopped	5
Lemon juice	15 ml/1 tbs
Oil	80 ml/⅓ cup
Red chilli powder	10 gms/2 tsp
Red chillies, whole	6
Salt to taste	
Tomatoes, skinned, chopped	350 gms/1¾ cups

Method:

Step 1. Heat the oil in a *kadhai*/wok, add the ginger and garlic pastes and sauté over medium heat for a minute.

2. Add the whole red chillies, garam masala, red chilli powder, lemon juice and tomatoes and sauté for 5 minutes until the gravy is smooth and well blended.

3. Add the green peas and stir. Season with salt and pepper.

To Serve:

Sprinkle cardamom powder, dry fenugreek leaves, crushed coriander seeds, green chillies and green coriander and serve hot with parantha or roti.

Vegetable Korma

A mixed vegetable stirred in cashewnut curry

Serves: 4-5   Preparation time: 10 minutes   Cooking time: 20 minutes

Ingredients:

Carrots, diced	120 gms/^{2}/$_3$ cup	Garlic paste	40 gms/2^2/$_3$ tbs
Cauliflower, cut into small flowerets	120 gms/^{2}/$_3$ cup	Ginger julienne	5 gms/1 tsp
French beans, 2 cm long	120 gms/^{2}/$_3$ cup	Ginger paste	40 gms/2^2/$_3$ tbs
Green peas	120 gms/^{2}/$_3$ cup	Green cardamoms	8
Mushrooms	120 gms/^{2}/$_3$ cup	Green chilli paste	25 gms/5 tsp
Potatoes, diced	120 gms/^{2}/$_3$ cup	Green coriander, chopped	15 gms/3 tsp
Bay leaf (tej patta)	1	Oil	60 ml/4 tbs
Cashewnuts or almonds	10	Onions, chopped	100 gms/½ cup
Cashewnut paste	100 gms/½ cup	Raisins	10
Cinnamon sticks	3	Salt to taste	
Cloves	6	White pepper	3 gms/^{2}/$_3$ tsp
Cream	60 ml/4 tbs	Yoghurt, whisked	200 gms/1 cup
Cumin seeds (jeera)	4 gms/¾ tsp		

Method:

Step 1. Heat a little oil in a pan. Lightly fry the cashewnuts (or almonds) and the raisins. Keep aside.

2. Parboil all the vegetables.

3. Heat the remaining oil. Add the cloves, cinnamon sticks, bay leaf, cumin seeds and green cardamoms and sauté until golden. Grind to a paste.

4. Add the ginger and garlic pastes, green chilli paste, cashewnut paste and the ground spices and cook until the oil separates from the gravy.

5. Add the yoghurt and cook on low heat for 5 minutes.

6. Add the parboiled vegetables, salt and white pepper. Cover and cook on low heat for 5-6 minutes.

7. Add the cream and transfer to a serving bowl.

To Serve:

Garnish with ginger juliennes, green coriander and the fried dried fruit.

Gobi Gulistan

Mattar Makhana Korma

Green peas and puffed lotus seeds cooked in green chilly and yoghurt curry

Serves: 4-5   Preparation time: 10 minutes   Cooking time: 25 minutes

Ingredients:

Green peas	600 gms	Ginger paste	40 gms/2²/₃ tbs
Makhana (puffed lotus seeds)	200 gms/1 cup	Green cardamoms	8
Bay leaf (tej patta)	1	Green chilli paste	25 gms/5 tsp
Butter	10 gms/2 tsp	Green coriander, chopped	15 gms/3 tsp
Cashewnut paste	100 gms/½ cup	Oil	60 ml/4 tbs
Cinnamon sticks	3	Onions, chopped	100 gms/½ cup
Cloves	10	Salt to taste	
Cream	60 ml/4 tbs	White pepper	3 gms/²/₃ tsp
Garlic paste	40 gms/2²/₃ tbs	Yoghurt	200 gms/1 cup
Ginger juliennes	5 gms/1 tsp		

Method:

Step 1. Parboil the green peas and the makhana.
  2. Heat the oil in a pan. Add cloves, cinnamon sticks, bay leaf and green cardamoms and sauté for 30 seconds. Add chopped onions and sauté until golden.
  3. Add the ginger and garlic pastes, green chilli paste and cashewnut paste and cook until the oil separates from the gravy.
  4. Add the yoghurt and cook on low heat for 5 minutes. Add the peas, makhana, salt and white pepper. Cover and cook on low heat for 5 minutes.
  5. Add the cream. Lightly fry the ginger juliennes in the butter.

To Serve:

Serve garnished with ginger juliennes and green coriander.

Palak Bhajee

Stir fried baby spinach with garlic and turmeric

Serves: 4-5   Preparation time: 10 minutes   Cooking time: 15 minutes

Ingredients:

Spinach (palak), fresh or frozen	1 kg	Red chillies, dried, cut in half	8
Asafoetida (heeng)	0.5 gm/¹/₈ tsp	Red chilli powder	5 gms/1 tsp
Garlic, peeled, cut lengthwise	60 gms/4 tbs	Salt to taste	
Oil	60 ml/4 tbs	Turmeric powder (haldi)	3 gms/²/₃ tsp
Onions, sliced or chopped	100 gms/½ cup		

Method:

Step 1. Wash the spinach leaves and chop roughly.
  2. Heat the oil in a wok/*kadhai* to smoking point. Reduce the heat, add the dry red chillies, onions, garlic, red chilli powder, turmeric powder and asafoetida and stir fry for 2-3 minutes.
  3. Immediately add the spinach leaves, toss and stir fry.
  4. Sprinkle with salt, cover and cook on very low heat for 6-7 minutes.

To Serve:

Serve hot with a dal, rice and rotis.

Palak Tomato Bhajee

Spinach leaves stirred in cumin and tomato gravy

Serves: 4-5   Preparation time: 10 minutes   Cooking time: 15 minutes

Ingredients:

Spinach (palak), fresh or frozen	1 kg	Oil	60 ml/4 tbs
Tomatoes, chopped	250 gms/1¼ cups	Onions, sliced or chopped	100 gms/½ cup
Asafoetida (heeng)	½ gms/⅛ tsp	Red chillies, dried, cut in half	8
Cumin seeds (jeera)	5 gms/1 tsp	Red chilli powder	5 gms/1 tsp
Garlic, peeled and cut lengthwise	60 gms/4 tbs	Salt to taste	
Ginger juliennes	10 gms/2 tsp	Turmeric powder (haldi)	3 gms/²⁄₃ tsp

Method:

Step 1. Wash the spinach and chop roughly.
   2. Heat the oil in a *kadhai*/wok to smoking point. Reduce heat, add the red chillies, cumin seeds, onions, garlic, red chilli powder, turmeric powder and asafoetida and stir fry for 2-3 minutes.
   3. Add chopped tomatoes and cook for 2 minutes.
   4. Immediately add the spinach, toss and stir fry. Sprinkle with salt, cover and cook over very low heat for 6-7 minutes.

To Serve:

Garnish with ginger juliennes and serve hot with a dal and rotis.

Palak Mushroom Bhajee

Spiced mushrooms with spinach leaves

Serves: 4-5   Preparation time: 10 minutes   Cooking time: 15 minutes

Ingredients:

Mushrooms, fresh or canned, sliced	200 gms/1 cup	Onions, sliced or chopped	100 gms/½ cup
Spinach (palak) leaves, washed and drained	1 kg	Red chillies, dried, cut in half	8
Asafoetida (heeng)	0.5 gms/⅛ tsp	Red chilli powder	5 gms/1 tsp
Garlic, peeled and cut into half lengthwise	60 gms/4 tbs	Refined oil	60 ml/4 tbs
		Salt to taste	
Ginger juliennes	10 gms/2 tsp	Turmeric powder (haldi)	3 gms/²⁄₃ tsp

Method:

Step 1. Wash the spinach thoroughly and chop roughly.
   2. Heat the oil in a *kadhai*/wok to smoking point. Add the red chillies, onions, garlic, red chilli powder, turmeric powder and asafoetida and stir fry on low heat for 2-3 minutes.
   3. Add the sliced mushrooms and cook for 2 minutes.
   4. Immediately add the spinach leaves, toss and stir fry.
   5. Sprinkle with salt, cover and cook over very low heat for 6-7 minutes. Season to taste.

To Serve:

Garnish with ginger juliennes and serve hot with a dal and rice or rotis.

Kadhai Mushroom

Mushrooms in a hot tomato curry

Serves: 4-5   Preparation time: 10 minutes   Cooking time: 15 minutes

Ingredients:

Mushrooms	800 gms	Green chillies, slit	6-8
Black pepper	6 gms/1¹/₃ tsp	Green coriander, chopped	15 gms/3 tsp
Coriander seeds, roasted and crushed	10 gms/2 tsp	Oil	60 ml/4 tbs
Fenugreek powder (methi)	3 gms/²/₃ tsp	Onions, chopped	100 gms/½ cup
Garam masala	15 gms/3 tsp	Red chillies, whole	10
Garlic paste	30 gms/6 tsp	Salt for seasoning	
Ginger paste	30 gms/6 tsp	Tomatoes, deseeded and skinned	350 gms/1¾ cups

Method:

Step 1. Trim, wash and cut the mushrooms into halves.

2. Heat the oil in a pan. Add the whole red chillies and chopped onions and sauté for 30 seconds. Add the ginger, garlic pastes and cook over medium heat.

3. Add the garam masala, fenugreek powder and tomatoes and cook over medium heat until the oil separates from the mixture.

4. Add mushrooms carefully and toss over high heat until mushrooms are well coated. Stirring occasionally, cook for 5-6 minutes.

5. Season with salt and sprinkle with crushed coriander seeds and black pepper.

To Serve:

Serve garnished with the green chillies and green coriander.

Kadhai Mushroom

Mushroom Jalfrezi

Mushroom and capsicum curry

Serves: 4-5   Preparation time: 10 minutes   Cooking time: 15 minutes

Ingredients:

Mushrooms (whole button mushrooms)	900 gms	Lemon juice	10 ml/2 tsp
Bay leaves (tej patta)	2	Oil	60 ml/4 tbs
Capsicum (green pepper), diced	150 gms/¾ cup	Onions, diced	150 gms/¾ cup
Cumin seeds (jeera)	3 gms/²⁄₃ tsp	Red chilli powder	5 gms/1 tsp
Garam masala	15 gms/3 tsp	Salt to taste	
Ginger juliennes	20 gms/4 tsp	Tomatoes, diced	150 gms/¾ cup
Green cardamoms	3	Turmeric powder (haldi)	8 gms/1²⁄₃ tsp
Green coriander, chopped	15 gms/3 tsp	Vinegar, white or malt	30 ml/2 tbs

Method:

Step 1. Heat the oil in a pan. Add the green cardamoms, bay leaves and cumin seeds and sauté over medium heat until they begin to crackle. Add turmeric powder and red chilli powder and sauté for 30 seconds.

2. Add the capsicum, onions and tomatoes and sauté for 30 seconds over high heat. Add the mushrooms, vinegar and garam masala and sauté for 30 seconds. Cover and cook for 6 minutes.

To Serve:

Season with salt and lemon juice. Garnish with ginger juliennes and green coriander.

Lazeez Khumb

Mushroom, capsicum and cabbage curry

Serves: 4-5   Preparation time: 10 minutes   Cooking time: 15 minutes

Ingredients:

Mushrooms, quartered	600 gms	Green chillies, chopped	4
Cabbage, shredded	120 gms/²⁄₃ cup	Green coriander, chopped	20 gms/4 tsp
Capsicum (green pepper), juliennes	60 gms/4 tbs	Oil	120 gms/²⁄₃ cup
Coriander seeds	5 gms/1 tsp	Onions, sliced	80 gms/¹⁄₃ cup
Garam masala	10 gms/2 tsp	Red chillies, whole	4
Garlic paste	20 gms/4 tsp	Salt to taste	
Ginger, chopped	30 gms/6 tsp	Tomatoes, chopped	500 gms/2½ cups

Method:

Step 1. Heat 2 tbs of oil in a *kadhai*/wok. Stir fry the quartered mushroom over medium heat for a few minutes. Remove and keep aside.

2. In the same oil stir fry the shredded cabbage until the liquid evaporates.

3. Pound the red chillies and coriander seeds with a pestle.

4. Heat the remaining oil in a *kadhai*/wok. Sauté the onions till they are transparent. Add the garlic paste and stir for 20 seconds over medium heat.

5. Add the pounded red chillies and coriander, garam masala and salt. Stir for 30 seconds. Add tomatoes and cook till the oil separates from the mixture.

6. Add the green chillies, ginger and half the green coriander and stir. Add the stir-fried mushroom and cabbage and cook for a few minutes.

To Serve:

Garnish with capsicum juliennes and the remaining green coriander. Serve with steamed rice or rotis.

Raseele Kum-Kum

Tomatoes stuffed with mushrooms

Serves: 4-5 | Preparation time: 15 minutes | Cooking time: 1 hour

Ingredients:

Mushrooms, chopped	500 gms/2½ cups
Tomatoes (firm and round)	15
Black cumin powder (shah jeera), roasted	2 gms/½ tsp
Garam masala	10 gms/2 tsp
Garlic, chopped	15 gms/3 tsp
Green chillies, finely chopped	5 gms/1 tsp
Green coriander, chopped	10 gms/2 tsp
Lemon juice	10 ml/2 tsp
Mint leaves, chopped	10 gms/2 tsp
Oil	30 ml/2 tbs
Onions, chopped	30 gms/2 tbs
Salt to taste	
Tomato pulp, fresh or canned	100 gms/½ cup
For the sauce:	
Bay leaf (tej patta)	1
Cream	60 ml/4 tbs
Garlic	10 gms/2 tsp
Green cardamoms	3 gms/2/3 tsp
Mace powder (javitri)	3 gms/2/3 tsp
Oil	25 ml/5 tsp
Onions, sliced	20 gms/4 tsp
Salt to taste	
Tomatoes, chopped	300 gms/1½ cups

Method:

Step 1. Slice off the tops of the tomatoes and scoop out the pulp. Keep aside the tomato shells and tops.

2. Heat the oil in a pan, sauté the onions, garlic and tomato pulp over medium heat until the moisture is completely evaporated and the oil separates from the gravy.
3. Add the green chillies and chopped mushrooms, stir and cook over high heat for 10-15 minutes till the water evaporates.
4. Add salt, garam masala, chopped mint leaves, lemon juice, cumin powder and half of the green coriander. Cool the mixture.
5. Fill each tomato with the mushroom mixture and cover with a tomato top. Bake the stuffed tomatoes in a greased baking tray for 15 minutes.
6. **For the sauce:** Heat oil in a pan. Sauté the cardamoms, bay leaf, onions, garlic and tomatoes. Then add 2 cups of water and salt and cook for about 30 minutes.
7. Strain through a fine sieve. Transfer the sauce to a saucepan and bring to a slow boil. Add cream and mace powder.

To Serve:

Pour the sauce over the baked tomatoes and sprinkle with the remaining half of the green coriander before serving.

Dhingri Shabnam

A delightful combination of mushroom and cottage cheese dumplings

Serves: 4-5 | Preparation time: 45 minutes | Cooking time: 30 minutes

Ingredients:

For the kofta:	
Cottage cheese (paneer)	300 gms/1½ cups
Flour	50 gms/¼ cup
Oil to deep fry koftas	120 ml/2/3 cup
For the filling:	
Butter	5 gms/1 tsp
Cashewnuts, chopped	8
Cottage cheese (paneer)	20 gms/4 tsp
Green chilli, deseeded and finely chopped	1
Green coriander, finely chopped	10 gms/2 tsp
Guchchi (morels) or button mushrooms	20 gms/4 tsp
Khoya (dried milk)	15 gms/3 tsp
Raisins	16
For the gravy:	
Cashewnut paste	40 gms/2 2/3 tbs
Fenugreek seeds (methi)	1 gm/¼ tsp
Garam masala	0.75 gms/¼ tsp
Garlic paste	10 gms/2 tsp
Ginger paste	10 gms/2 tsp
Oil	60 ml/4 tbs
Onions, chopped	50 gms/¼ cup
Onion paste, fried	20 gms/4 tsp
Red chilli powder	0.75 gms/¼ tsp
Salt to taste	
Turmeric powder (haldi)	0.75 gms/¼ tsp
Yoghurt	75 gms/1/3 cup

Method:

Step 1. **For the kofta:** Mash 200 gms (1 cup) of paneer in a bowl. Add flour and mix to make a dough. Divide into 8 equal portions and shape into balls.

2. **For the filling:** Soak the guchchi in lukewarm water for 5 minutes. Drain, wash in running water for 2-3 minutes and then soak in water until they become soft and swollen. Drain, squeeze out the excess water, remove stems and slice thin.

3. Melt the butter in a pan, add the guchchi and sauté over medium heat for 30 seconds.

4. Add the khoya and fry over medium heat until light golden. Add chopped cashewnuts and raisins.

5. Mash the remaining paneer in a bowl, add the guchchi, khoya and the remaining ingredients and mix well. Divide into 8 equal portions.

6. Flatten the kofta balls and place a portion of the filling in the middle of each and round off again.

7. Heat the oil in a *kadhai*/wok, and deep fry the koftas until light golden. Remove and keep aside.

8. **For the gravy:** Heat the oil in a *kadhai*/wok. Add fenugreek seeds and sauté over medium heat until they begin to crackle.

9. Add chopped onions and sauté until light golden. Add the garlic, ginger pastes, fry for a minute, and then add the turmeric, red chilli powder and salt and stir.

10. Add the cashewnut paste and yoghurt and fry until the oil separates from the gravy.

11. Add the fried onion paste and stir. Add 4½ cups of water, bring to a boil and then simmer until the gravy has the consistency of a sauce.

12. Remove and strain the gravy through a soup strainer into another pan. Return the strained gravy to the heat, gently add the koftas to the gravy and simmer for 5 minutes.

13. Sprinkle with garam masala and stir.

To Serve:

Transfer to a bowl and serve with pulao or phulka.

Anjeeri Kum-Kum

Delicious mushrooms stuffed with figs—an ideal starter!

Serves: 4-5   Preparation time: 45 minutes
Cooking time: 5 minutes

Ingredients:

Dried figs	300 gms/1½ cups
Mushrooms (approximately 30)	600 gms/3 cups
Garam masala	4 gms/¾ tsp
Garlic, grated	3 gms/⅔ tsp
Ginger, grated	3 gms/⅔ tsp
Green chillies	5 gms/1 tsp
Lemon juice	5 ml/1 tsp
Milk, to dissolve saffron	10 ml/2 tsp
Onions, grated	10 gms/2 tsp
Refined oil	10 ml/2 tsp
Saffron	2 gms
Salt to taste	
White pepper powder	2 gms/½ tsp

Raseele Kum-Kum

Method:

Step 1. Soak the dried figs in lukewarm water for 20 minutes. Drain, wipe and chop to make a paste. Add all the other ingredients, except the mushrooms, oil, milk and saffron. Season to taste.

2. Stuff each mushroom with 8-10 gms of the mixture and keep aside for 20 minutes.

3. In a pan, heat the oil till moderately hot. Arrange the mushrooms in the pan and let them cook on low heat for 1-1½ minutes. Turn the mushrooms over and cook for another minute.

To Serve:

Remove the mushrooms from pan, brush with saffron dissolved in milk and serve immediately.

NOTE: The mushrooms can also be placed on a greased baking dish and baked in a moderately hot oven for 5 minutes.

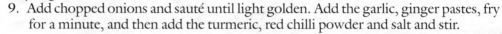

Dum ke Baigan

Aubergines cooked on a slow fire

Serves: 4-5   Preparation time: 10 minutes   Cooking time: 45 minutes

Ingredients:

Aubergines (baigan), small, oval/round ones	800 gms/20	Green cardamoms	10
Bay leaf (tej patta)	1	Green coriander, chopped	15 gms/3 tsp
Black peppercorn	6 gms/1⅓ tsp	Oil	120 ml/⅔ cup
Cinnamon sticks	5	Onion paste	150 gms/¾ cup
Cloves	10	Red chillies, whole	12
Cumin seeds (jeera)	10 gms/2 tsp	Salt to taste	
Garlic paste	40 gms/2⅔ tbs	Turmeric powder (haldi)	5 gms/1 tsp
Ginger paste	40 gms/2⅔ tbs	Vinegar, malt	60 ml/4 tbs

Method:

Step 1. Trim the stems of the aubergines. Slit open each aubergine crosswise, without disjointing it from the stem.

2. In a pan heat 1 tbs of oil over medium heat. Add the red chillies, cumin seeds, black peppercorn, green cardamoms, cinnamon sticks, bay leaf, cloves and cumin seed and sauté over medium heat for 5-6 minutes. Cool and grind to a fine powder.

3. Mix in vinegar to make a fine paste.

4. Heat a little oil in a pan. Fry the aubergines, a few at a time, for 5-6 minutes or until they are half cooked. Remove from the heat and keep aside.

5. In the same pan, heat the remaining oil, add the onion paste and sauté over medium heat for 10-12 minutes, until the paste is lightly coloured.

6. Add the ginger and garlic pastes, turmeric powder and the ground spice paste. Stir and cook over medium heat for 4-5 minutes.

7. Add the salt and two-thirds cup of hot water and cook until the water evaporates and the oil separates from the sauce.

8. Arrange the fried aubergines in the sauce, stir very carefully, cover and cook on *dum* (over a low flame or in a slow oven) for 3-4 minutes.

To Serve:

Garnish with green coriander.

NOTE: For round, large seedless aubergines, slice with the skin, 2 cm thick, and follow the same method.

Baigan ka Bharta

A charcoal smoked aubergine delicacy

Serves: 4-5   Preparation time: 20 minutes   Cooking time: 20 minutes

Ingredients:

Aubergines (baigan), large, round ones	1 kg	Onions, chopped	120 gms/⅔ cup
Cumin seeds (jeera)	3 gms/⅔ tsp	Paprika powder	5 gms/1 tsp
Ginger, chopped	10 gms/2 tsp	Salt to taste	
Green chillies	2	Tomatoes, chopped	400 gms/2 cups
Green coriander, chopped	15 gms/3 tsp	Yoghurt	150 gms/¾ cup
Oil	150 gms/¾ cup		

Method:

Step 1. Preheat the oven to 175°C (350°F). Skewer the aubergines, baste with a little oil and roast in an oven until the skin starts peeling off. This process can also be performed on a charcoal grill or over a low flame. Immerse the aubergines in water to cool. Remove the skin and the stem and chop the flesh roughly.

2. Heat the oil in a *kadhai*/wok, add cumin seeds and sauté over medium heat until they begin to crackle.

3. Add onions and sauté until brown. Add the ginger and stir. Reduce the heat, add yoghurt, paprika and salt and stir.

4. Add the tomatoes and sauté until the oil starts separating from the gravy.

5. Add the chopped aubergines and sauté for 4-5 minutes. Add green chillies and stir.

To Serve:

Serve hot or cold, garnished with green coriander leaves.

Baghar-e-Baigan

Aubergines from the court of the Nizam of Hyderabad

Serves: 4-5   Preparation time: 10 minutes   Cooking time: 20 minutes

Ingredients:

Aubergines (baigan), medium	½ kg/500 gms	Ginger paste	30 gms/2 tbs
Coconut, desiccated	15 gms/3 tsp	Oil	200 gms/1 cup
Coriander powder	15 gms/3 tsp	Onions, chopped	200 gms/1 cup
Cumin powder (jeera)	10 gms/2 tsp	Red chilli powder	15 gms/2 tsp
Curry leaves	3	Salt to taste	
Fenugreek seeds (methi)	1 gm/¼ tsp	Sesame seeds (til)	15 gms/3 tsp
Garlic cloves, chopped	30 gms/2 tbs	Tamarind (imli)	50 gms/3⅓ tbs
Garlic paste	30 gms/2 tbs	Turmeric powder (haldi)	5 gms/1 tsp

Method:

Step 1. Soak the tamarind in warm water and squeeze out the pulp.
2. Cut the aubergines into 4 without disjointing them from the stem.
3. Grind the onions and ginger and garlic pastes to a fine mixture.
4. Roast the sesame seeds, coconut, chilli powder and coriander powder. Add 15 ml of water and grind to a fine paste.
5. Heat the oil, add curry leaves, the cumin, fenugreek and few cloves of garlic and sauté in heated oil for the *baghar* (tempering).
6. Now put all the ground spices, aubergines, half a cup of water and tamarind pulp, turmeric powder and salt in a pan with the *baghar* and cook on a low fire till the aubergines become tender.

To Serve:

Serve with steamed rice.

Vegetable Pakoras

Assorted vegetable fritters

Serves: 4-5   Preparation time: 20 minutes   Cooking time: 15 minutes

Ingredients:

Aubergines (baigan), cut into small pieces	150 gms/¾ cup	Baking soda	2-3 gms/½-⅔ tsp
Capsicum (green pepper), cut into long strips	150 gms/¾ cup	Black cumin seeds (shah jeera)	6 gms/1⅓ tsp
		Carom seeds (ajwain)	3 gms/⅔ tsp
Cauliflower, cut into small pieces	150 gms/¾ cup	Gram flour (besan)	200 gms/1 cup
Onions, thick, round slices	150 gms/¾ cup	Red chilli powder	6 gms/1⅓ tsp
Potatoes, cut into small pieces	150 gms/¾ cup	Refined oil	750 ml/3¾ cups
Spinach (palak) leaves	150 gms/¾ cup	Salt to taste	
		Water	100 ml/½ cup

Method:

Step 1. In a bowl sieve the gram flour, baking soda and salt. Add the red chilli powder and water to make a thin batter.
2. Add carom seeds.
3. Heat the oil in a *kadhai*/wok. Dip one kind of vegetable at a time in the batter and fry in the hot oil over medium heat until golden and crisp.
4. Remove from the oil and drain on an absorbent kitchen towel.

To Serve:

Serve hot with mint chutney.

NOTE: The vegetables can be mixed in the batter and fried, or individual vegetables could be fried and served separately.

Punjabi Chana Masala

Bengal gram curry

Serves: 4-5   Preparation time: 45 minutes   Cooking time: 1 hour

Ingredients:

Bengal gram (chana), split	250 gms/1¼ cups	Ginger paste	10 gms/2 tsp
Bay leaf (tej patta)	1	Green coriander, chopped	5 gms/1 tsp
Butter	40 gms/2²/₃ tbs	Onions, chopped	100 gms/½ cup
Cinnamon stick	1	Salt to taste	
Garam masala	6 gms/1¹/₃ tsp	Tomatoes, skinned and chopped	60 gms/4 tbs
Garlic paste	10 gms/2 tsp	Water	1.5 litres/7½ cups

Method:

Step 1. Clean the chana, wash in water 3 or 4 times and soak for 30 minutes in a bowl of water.

2. Boil water in a saucepan. Add the bay leaf, cinnamon stick and the drained chana, and bring back to a slow boil. Remove the scum from the top of the pan and simmer until the chana is completely cooked and tender. Discard the bay leaf and cinnamon sticks from the chana.

3. Heat the butter in a large saucepan and sauté the onions till they are soft and golden. Add the garam masala, ginger, garlic pastes and sauté over medium heat for 2-3 minutes.

4. Add the tomatoes, cooked chana and salt to the saucepan, cover and cook for another 2-3 minutes.

To Serve:

Serve hot garnished with green coriander.

NOTE: Boiled potatoes (200 gms/1 cup) tossed in butter (30 gms/2 tbs) could be added with lemon juice (15 ml/1 tbs).

Chana Pindi

Chick-pea curry

Serves: 4-5   Preparation time: 3 hours 15 minutes   Cooking time: 1 hour

Ingredients:

Chick peas (kabuli chana), whole	250 gms/1¼ cups	Oil	60 gms/4 tbs
Baking soda	5-6 gms/1-1¹/₃ tsp	Red chilli powder	4 gms/¾ tsp
Bay leaf (tej patta)	1	Salt for seasoning	
Cardamoms, green or black	3	Tea-bag	1
Chana masala (aromatic garam masala)	5 gms/1 tsp		
Cinnamon sticks	3	**For garnish:**	
Coriander powder	5 gms/1 tsp	Green chillies, whole	10
Garam masala	5 gms/1 tsp	Lemons, cut into wedges	3
Garlic paste	10 gms/2 tsp	Onion rings	100 gms/½ cup
Ginger paste	10 gms/2 tsp	Tomatoes, medium quartered	60 gms/4 tbs
Lemon juice	15 ml/1 tbs		

Method:

Step 1. Clean, wash and soak the kabuli chana in water for 3 hours.

2. In a heavy pot boil 2 litres of water, add the bay leaf, cinnamon sticks, cardamoms, tea-bag and kabuli chana, and bring back to boil. Add baking soda. Cover and cook over low heat until the kabuli chana is soft. Drain immediately. Remove the bay leaf, tea-bag, cinnamon sticks and cardamoms.

3. Heat the oil in a pan over low heat. Add the ginger and garlic pastes and sauté for 30-40 seconds. Add the red chilli powder, garam masala, coriander powder, chana masala , salt and lemon juice.

4. Add the cooked chanas, mixing carefully.

To Serve:

Garnish with the onion rings, whole green chillies and tomatoes, with lemon wedges on the sides.
Serve with pooris or bhaturas or kulchas or even bread slices.

Dal Amritsari

A staple in all homes across north India, a necessary part of every vegetarian meal

Serves: 4-5   Preparation time: 45 minutes   Cooking time: 1 hour

Ingredients:

Black beans (urad dal), split and husked	250 gms/1¼ cups	Green chillies	2
Chick peas (chana dal), split	80 gms/⅓ cup	Mint leaves, chopped	5 gms/1 tsp
Butter	120 gms/⅔ cup	Oil	100 ml/½ cup
Garlic paste	20 gms/4 tsp	Onions, chopped	50 gms/¼ cup
Ginger paste	20 gms/4 tsp	Salt to taste	
		Tomatoes, chopped	150 gms/¾ cup

Method:

Step 1. Wash the dals in running water and soak for at least 30 minutes. Drain the dals.

2. In a saucepan put 2 litres of water, salt and the dals. Bring to a boil, reduce the heat and simmer. Remove the scum that collects on top of the pan.

3. Add two-thirds of the ginger and garlic pastes, cover and simmer until the dals are cooked and two-thirds of the liquid has evaporated.

4. Mash the dals lightly against the sides of the pan with a wooden spoon.

5. Heat the oil in a pan. Add the onions and sauté over medium heat until light brown. Add the remaining ginger, garlic pastes and sauté until the onions are brown.

6. Add the green chillies, stir for a minute, then add the tomatoes and butter. Cook until tomatoes are mashed.

7. Add the lightly mashed dals to this mixture. Stir for few minutes, until the dal has a medium thick consistency.

To Serve:

Garnish with chopped mint leaves. Serve with boiled rice or with a vegetable preparation and rotis.

Dal Sultani

A dal seasoned with saffron, fit for a sultan

Serves: 4-5   Preparation time: 40 minutes   Cooking time: 30 minutes

Ingredients:

Pigeon peas (toovar dal)	250 gms/1¼ cups	Red chilli powder	10 gms/2 tsp
Black cumin seeds (shah jeera)	5 gms/1 tsp	Saffron (soaked in cream)	1 gm
Butter	50 gms/¼ cup	Salt to taste	
Cream	30 ml/2 tbs	Turmeric powder (haldi)	5 gms/1 tsp
Onions, quartered	150 gms/¾ cup		

Method:

Step 1. Wash the dal 3 or 4 times in running water and soak for half an hour in cold water.

2. In a heavy pan bring 2 litres of water to a boil. Add the dal and return to a boil. Remove the scum that collects on top of the pan.

3. Reduce the heat. Add two-thirds of the turmeric powder, cover and cook until the dal is completely soft. Add salt.

4. In a separate pan, heat butter on a low flame. Add onions and sauté over medium heat. Add the cumin seeds, the remaining turmeric powder and red chilli powder and stir. When the seeds begin to sizzle, immediately add the cooked dal to this pan.

5. Cover and cook for 2-3 minutes.

To Serve:

Pour the cream and saffron mixture over the dal and serve with boiled rice.

Mahi Tikka   80

Tandoori Lobster   77

Jhinga Nisha   76

Zafrani Mahi Kebab   78

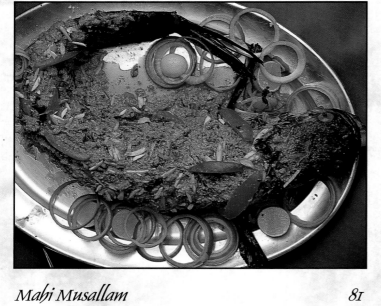

Mahi Musallam   81

Tandoori Fish Gulnar   77

Fish & Seafood

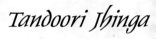

Tandoori Jhinga

Grilled king prawns

Serves: 4-5   Preparation time: 3 hours   Cooking time: 20 minutes

Ingredients:

King prawns (10)	1 kg	Garlic paste	30 gms/2 tbs
Black pepper, crushed	3 gms/^{2}/$_3$ tsp	Ginger paste	30 gms/2 tbs
Butter for basting	50 gms/3^1/$_3$ tbs	Green chilli paste	10 gms/2 tsp
Carom seeds (ajwain)	5 gms/1 tsp	Lemon juice	15 ml/1 tbs
Cornflour	25 gms/1^2/$_3$ tbs	Saffron (dissolved in 15 ml milk)	1 gm
Cream	30 ml/2 tbs	Salt to taste	
Egg	1		

Method:

Step 1. Marinate the prawns in the lemon juice and salt mixture for 1 hour.
2. In a bowl combine all the other ingredients, except the butter, into a fine batter.
3. Dip the prawns in this batter and marinate for 2 hours.
4. Heat the oven to 175 °C (350 °F).
5. Skewer the prawns, 2 cm apart. Roast the prawns in an oven or hot tandoor or over a charcoal grill for 10 minutes.
6. Hang the skewer to drain off the moisture for a few minutes.
7. Baste with butter and roast again for 3-4 minutes.

To Serve:

Serve with mint chutney, salads and roti.

Jhinga Nisha

An exotic starter, prawns flavoured with sesame seeds and fenugreek!

Serves: 4-5   Preparation time: 1½ hours   Cooking time: 20 minutes

Ingredients:

Large prawns	8	Ginger paste	10 gms/2 tsp
Chaat masala	5 gms/1 tsp	Green chillies	5 gms/6
Cheddar cheese	15 gms/3 tsp	Lemon juice	5 ml/1 tsp
Cinnamon powder	5 gms/1 tsp	Salt to taste	
Clove powder	5 gms/1 tsp	Sesame seeds (til)	15 gms/3 tsp
Fenugreek (kasoori methi)	5 gms/1 tsp	White pepper powder	5 gms/1 tsp
Garlic paste	10 gms/2 tsp	Yoghurt	20 gms/4 tsp

Method:

Step 1. Rub the lemon juice, ginger and garlic pastes and salt on the prawns and keep aside for half an hour.
2. Roast the sesame seeds slightly and crush them to a powder.
3. Beat the yoghurt in a bowl and add the remaining ingredients (except for the chaat masala and lemon juice).
4. Rub this mixture onto each prawn and keep in a cool place for 1 hour.
5. Preheat the oven to 150 °C (300 °F).
6. Skewer the prawns and roast in the oven till light golden in colour.
7. Press the sesame seed powder over the prawns and roast again for 2 minutes.

To Serve:

Sprinkle with chaat masala and lemon juice. Garnish with onion rings.

Patrani Machchi

Patrani machchi is a Parsi delicacy cooked without any fat. No Parsi banquet is complete without it

Serves: 4-5   Preparation time: 45 minutes   Cooking time: 15 minutes

Ingredients:

Fish fillet	1 kg	Cumin seeds (jeera)	15 gms/3 tsp
Banana leaves or aluminium foil		Fresh coconut, grated	100 gms/½ cup
Lemon juice	25 ml/5 tsp	Garlic	20 gms/4 tsp
Oil	30 ml/2 tbs	Green chillies	6
Salt to taste		Green coriander, chopped	15 gms/3 tsp
Vinegar, malt	90 ml/⅓ cup	Red chilli powder	5 gms/1 tsp
For the green coconut chutney:		Sugar	25 gms/5 tsp
Coriander seeds	50 gms/3⅓ tbs		

Method:

Step 1. Marinate the fish fillets in vinegar, lemon juice and salt for 30 minutes.
2. Trim, wash and wipe the banana leaves.
3. Combine all the ingredients for the green chutney with a little water in a blender to make a fine paste:
4. Apply this paste liberally to the fish fillets.
5. Apply the oil to the banana leaves and wrap each fillet separately in them. Alternately, wrap each fillet in foil.
6. Steam the fish in a steamer for 10-15 minutes.

To Serve:

Unwrap the fish, arrange on a platter and serve with lemon wedges.

Tandoori Lobster

A spectacular party special!

Serves: 4-5   Preparation time: 4½ hours   Cooking time: 10 minutes

Ingredients:

Lobster (medium)	4	Gram flour (besan)	50 gms/3⅓ tbs
Butter for basting	100 gms/½ cup	Vinegar, malt	120 ml/⅔ cup
Carom seeds (ajwain)	3 gms/⅔ tsp	Mustard oil (sarson ka tel)	50 ml/4 tbs
Cottage cheese (paneer)	50 gms/¼ cup	Red chilli paste	5 gms/ 1 tsp
Egg	1	Salt to taste	
Garam masala	10 gms/2 tsp	White pepper powder	5 gms/1 tsp
Garlic paste	20 gms/4 tsp	Yoghurt, hung	200 gms/1 cup
Ginger paste	20 gms/4 tsp		

Method:

Step 1. Cut each lobster shell into half and then shell and devein the lobster. Wash the shells and reserve. Dry and dip the shells in hot oil and keep aside.
2. Marinate the lobsters in a mixture made of ginger and garlic pastes, ajwain, vinegar and salt. Keep aside for 1 hour.
3. Whisk the yoghurt in a large bowl, add the remaining ingredients and rub the lobsters with this mixture. Keep aside for 3 hours.
4. Skewer the lobsters 2 cm apart. Keep a tray underneath to collect the excess drippings.
5. Roast in a moderately hot tandoor or preheated oven to 175 °C (350 °F) for 5 minutes.
6. Baste with butter and cook again for 2 minutes.

To Serve:

Place on a platter; garnish with lettuce, tomatoes, onion rings and salad ingredients. Serve the lobster placed on the shell.

Tandoori Fish Gulnar

Broiled whole fish with the delicate flavour of carom

Serves: 4-5   Preparation time: 1½ hours   Cooking time: 15 minutes

Ingredients:

Fish (pomfret/sole/bhetki), 450 gms each	4	Lemon juice	40 ml/2⅔ tbs
Butter for basting	50 gms/¼ cup	Red chilli powder	4 gms/¾ tsp
Carom seeds (ajwain)	10 gms/2 tsp	Salt to taste	
Cream	40 ml/2⅔ tbs	Turmeric powder (haldi)	4 gms/¾ tsp
Egg, beaten	1	Vinegar, malt	120 ml/⅔ cup
Garlic paste	20 gms/4 tsp	White pepper powder	3 gms/⅔ tsp
Ginger paste	10 gms/2 tsp	Yoghurt, hung	20 gms/4 tsp
Gram flour (besan)	25 gms/5 tsp		

Method:

Step 1. Wash and clean the fish. Make three incisions on each side.
2. Mix the vinegar, lemon juice, half the garlic paste, half the chilli powder and salt. Marinate the fish in this mixture for half an hour.
3. Whisk the yoghurt and add the egg and the remaining ingredients to it. Mix well.
4. Remove the fish from the first marinade. Hold aloft to allow excess marinade to drip off and transfer the fish to the second marinade for at least 1 hour.
5. Skewer the fish from mouth to tail 2 cm apart and bake in a moderately hot oven for 8 minutes. (Alternately, grill the fish, turning once.)
6. Remove and hang the skewer to allow the excess moisture to drip off.
7. Baste with butter and roast or grill for a further 3 minutes.

To Serve:

Remove the fish from the skewers and serve hot, garnished with onion rings and lemon slices/wedges.

Tandoori Bharwan Jalpari

Stuffed whole grilled/baked fish

Serves: 4-5   Preparation time: 3½ hours   Cooking time: 20 minutes

Ingredients:

River or sea fish (with single centre bone), 400 gms each	5	Gram flour (besan)	40 gms/2²/₃ tbs
Black pepper powder	10 gms/2 tsp	Lemon juice	25 ml/5 tsp
Butter to baste	50 gms/3¹/₃ tbs	Red chilli powder	20 gms/4 tsp
Fennel seed (saunf)	10 gms/2 tsp	Salt to taste	
Garlic paste	25 gms/5 tsp	Turmeric powder (haldi)	10 gms/2 tsp
Ghee (clarified butter)	50 ml/3¹/₃ tbs	Vinegar, malt	45 ml/3 tbs
Ginger paste	25 gms/5 tsp	Yoghurt, hung	200 gms/1 cup

Method:

Step 1. Marinate fish in vinegar and half the salt.
  2. In a bowl, combine all the remaining ingredients and mix to a fine paste.
  3. Rub the paste inside and outside the fish and let it stand for 2-3 hours.
  4. Preheat the oven to 175 °C (350 °F).
  5. Skewer the fish from tail to mouth, 4 cms apart.
  6. Roast in the oven for 12-15 minutes. Keep a tray underneath to collect the drippings.
  7. Baste with butter. Remove and hang the skewers and let the excess moisture drip off.

To Serve:

Serve with mint chutney, garnished with sliced cucumbers, tomatoes and onion rings.

Zafrani Mahi Kebab

Fish patties flavoured with sesame

Serves: 4-5   Preparation time: 45 minutes
          Cooking time: 15 minutes

Ingredients:

Fish (any white fish), boneless	900 gms
Chaat masala	5 gms/1 tsp
Cream	30 ml/2 tbs
Egg, white only	1
Eggs, beaten	3
Garam masala	5 gms/1 tsp
Garlic paste	40 gms/2²/₃ tbs
Ginger paste	40 gms/2²/₃ tbs
Gram flour (besan) or white flour	60 gms/4 tbs
Green chillies, chopped	6 gms/3
Green coriander, chopped	10 gms/2 tsp
Lemon juice	45 ml/3 tbs
Mace powder (javitri)	3 gms/²/₃ tsp
Oil for frying	200 ml/1 cup
Saffron strands	2 gms/½ tsp
Salt to taste	

| Sesame seeds (til) | 60 gms/4 tbs | White pepper powder | 5 gms/1 tsp |
| Vetivier (kewda) | 3 drops | Yellow chilli powder (deghi mirch) | 6 gms/1¹/₃ tsp |

Method:

Step 1. Boil the fish. Make sure that there are no bones and mince it well.
2. In a bowl, mix all the ingredients, except the sesame seeds and egg white, with the minced fish.
3. Divide the mixture into 20 equal portions and shape into round balls. Press each ball between the palms to make a patty, approximately 6 cm in diameter.
4. Beat the egg white lightly.
5. Coat each patty with the egg white, sprinkle sesame seed evenly on top.
6. Heat the oil and shallow fry each patty until golden.

To Serve:

Arrange the patties on a serving platter and sprinkle the chaat masala. Serve with sliced cucumbers, tomatoes, lemon wedges and mint chutney.

Goan Prawn Curry

A taste of Goa in this curry made with coconut milk

Serves: 4-5   Preparation time: 20 minutes   Cooking time: 20 minutes

Ingredients:

Prawns	1 kg	Oil	120 ml/²/₃ cup
Coconut milk	100 ml/½ cup	Onion paste	100 gms/½ cup
Coriander seeds	15 gms/3 tsp	Red chillies, whole	15
Cumin seeds (jeera)	5 gms/1 tsp	Salt to taste	
Garlic paste	30 gms/6 tsp	Tamarind (imli)	40 gms/2²/₃ tbs
Ginger paste	30 gms/6 tsp	Tomatoes	150 gms/¾ cup
Green chillies	5	Turmeric powder (haldi)	5 gms/1 tsp
Green coriander, chopped	5 gms/1 tsp		

Method:

Step 1. Shell, devein and pat the prawns dry.
2. Dissolve the tamarind in half a cup of hot water for about 20 minutes. Strain all the pulp out of the tamarind.
3. Put the garlic, ginger, cumin seeds, turmeric, coriander seeds and tamarind pulp into a blender. Add 90 ml of water and blend into a fine paste.
4. Heat the oil in a pan. Add the red chillies and sauté for 30 seconds. Add the onion paste and sauté over medium heat until golden brown. Add tomatoes, salt and the blended paste and cook for 2 minutes.
5. Add half the coconut milk and 1 cup of water and bring to a boil.
6. Add prawns and cook for 5 minutes.
7. Add the remaining coconut milk and bring to a boil.

To Serve:

Garnish with green chillies and green coriander. Serve with rice.

Goan Prawn Curry

Mahi Tikka

Char broiled fish cubes

Serves: 4-5   Preparation time: 3-4 hours   Cooking time: 20 minutes

Ingredients:

River fish (with single bone in centre), cut into 4 cm cubes	800 gms	Ginger paste	40 gms/2²/₃ tbs
Butter for basting	50 gms/3¹/₃ tbs	Green chilli paste	15 gms/3 tsp
Cottage cheese (paneer), grated	50 gms/3¹/₃ tbs	Lemon juice	20 ml/4 tsp
Fresh mint paste	10 gms/2 tsp	Salt to taste	
Garam masala	10 gms/2 tsp	White pepper	5 gms/1 tsp
		Yoghurt , hung	200 gms/1 cup

Method:

Step 1. Marinate the fish cubes in salt and lemon juice for 1 hour in the refrigerator.
2. In a bowl, combine all the other ingredients and whisk to a creamy batter.
3. Marinate the fish cubes in the batter for at least 2-3 hours.
4. Heat the oven to 175 °C (350 °F).
5. Skewer the fish cubes, 5 pieces on each skewer, 2 cm apart, and roast in the oven, tandoor or open charcoal grill or 8-10 minutes.
6. Baste fish with butter.
7. Roast for a further 2-3 minutes.

To Serve:

Serve with sliced onions, tomatoes, sliced cucumber and mint chutney.

Fish Amritsari

A spicy cuisine from Amritsar in the Punjab

Serves: 4-5   Preparation time: 2-4 hours   Cooking time: 15 minutes

Ingredients:

Fish (steak or fillet), with or without bone	1 kg	Oil	200 ml/1 cup
Carom seeds (ajwain)	10 gms/2 tsp	Red chilli powder	8 gms/1²/₃ tsp
Chaat masala	6 gms/1¹/₃ tsp	Salt for seasoning	
Garlic paste	60 gms/4 tbs	Turmeric powder (haldi)	8 gms/1²/₃ tsp
Ginger paste	60 gms/4 tbs	Vinegar, white	50 ml/¼ cup
Gram flour (besan) or white flour	120 gms/²/₃ cup	White pepper powder	8 gms/1²/₃ tsp
Lemon juice	50 ml/4 tbs		

Method:

Step 1. Clean, wash and dry the fish.
2. Prick each piece of fish with a sharp fork. Carefully marinate the fish fillet with salt and two-thirds of the vinegar and let them stand for 1-2 hours.
3. In a bowl mix all the dry ingredients, with the ginger and garlic pastes, lemon juice, the remaining vinegar and salt to a creamy batter.
4. Dip each piece of fish in this batter. Arrange the pieces on a flat tray and let them stand for 1-2 hours at room temperature.
5. Heat the oil in a heavy pan or frying pan over medium heat. Shallow fry the fish till golden and crisp. Drain the fish on kitchen towels.

To Serve:

Sprinkle the fish with chaat masala and serve, accompanied by sliced cucumbers, tomatoes, lemon wedges and mint chutney.

Mahi Musallam

A whole large fish smothered in cashewnut and fenugreek (methi)

Serves: 4-5   Preparation time: 25 minutes   Cooking time: 1 hour

Ingredients:

River or sea fish (whole)	2 kg	Salt to taste	
Butter, melted	30 gms/2 tbs	Turmeric powder (haldi)	10 gms/2 tsp
Cashewnut paste	100 gms/½ cup	Vetivier (kewda)	5 drops
Coriander powder	15 gms/3 tsp	Yoghurt	180 gms/¾ cup
Fenugreek powder (methi)	6 gms/1⅓ tsp		
Garam masala	15 gms/3 tsp	**For the marinade paste:**	
Garlic paste	50 gms/3⅓ tbs	Garlic paste	20 gms/4 tsp
Ginger paste	50 gms/3⅓ tbs	Ginger paste	20 gms/4 tsp
Lemon juice	15 ml/1 tbs	Lemon juice	15 ml/1 tbs
Oil	200 ml/1 cup	Red chilli powder	5 gms/1 tsp
Onion paste	200 gms/1 cup	Salt to taste	
Red chilli powder	10 gms/2 tsp		

Method:

Step 1. Clean, wash and wipe the fish thoroughly.
    2. Mix all the ingredients for the marinade. Prick the fish with a sharp fork, rub the marinade all over and leave aside for 1 hour.
    3. Heat the oil in a pan to smoking point. Arrange the fish in a baking dish. Baste the fish with hot oil until the fish is half cooked.
    4. To the oil left in the pan add onion paste, ginger and garlic pastes and cashewnut paste and stir. Add coriander powder, red chilli powder, turmeric powder and salt.
    5. Add the yoghurt, bring the mixture to a boil, reduce to medium heat and stir until the oil separates from the mixture.
    6. Add hot water (about 1½ cups) and bring it to a slow boil. Add fenugreek powder, garam masala and vetivier.
    7. Preheat the oven to 120 °C (250 °F). Pour the hot gravy over the fish and bake for 40 minutes. At intervals of 15 minutes baste the fish with the gravy.

To Serve:

Remove the fish gently and arrange carefully in a shallow dish. Strain the gravy and add the lemon juice. Pour the gravy over the fish and garnish with chopped green coriander and melted butter. Serve with plain rice or pooris.

Fried Fish

A ginger flavoured spiced fried fish

Serves: 4-5   Preparation time: 2 hours   Cooking time: 15 minutes

Ingredients:

Fish, cut into 5 cm X 5 cm or 2" square thin slices	1 kg	Lemon juice	25 ml/5 tsp
		Red chilli powder	8 gms/1⅔ tsp
Carom seeds (ajwain)	10 gms/2 tsp	Refined oil	500 ml/2½ cups
Chaat masala	6 gms/1⅓ tsp	Salt to taste	
Garlic paste	60 gms/4 tbs	Turmeric powder (haldi)	8 gms/1⅔ tsp
Ginger paste	60 gms/4 tbs	White pepper powder	8 gms/1⅔ tsp
Gram flour (besan)	120 gms/⅔ cup	White vinegar	50 gms/¼ cup

Method:

Step 1. Prick fish with a sharp fork.
    2. Rub salt and lemon juice over the fish pieces and keep aside for 1-2 hours.
    3. In bowl mix all the other ingredients except the chaat masala and oil.
    4. Dip each fish piece in the batter and let them stand for another half an hour.
    5. Heat the oil in a *kadhai*/wok and deep fry the fish pieces over medium heat.

To Serve:

Sprinkle the fish with chaat masala and serve accompanied by sliced cucumbers, tomatoes, lemon wedges and green chutney.

Naan

Leavened bread

Serves: 4-5   Preparation time: 3 hours   Cooking time: 20 minutes

Ingredients:

Plain flour	500 gms/2½ cups	Milk	50 ml/3⅓ tbs
Baking powder	5 gms/1 tsp	Oil/ghee (clarified butter)	25 gms/5 tsp
Baking soda	1 gm/⅕ tsp	Onion seed (kalonji)	3 gms/⅔ tsp
Egg	1	Salt to taste	
Flour to dust as required		Sugar	10 gms/2 tsp
Ghee to grease the baking tray		Water	250 ml/1¼ cups
Melon seeds	5 gms/1 tsp		

Method:

Step 1. Sieve the flour, salt, baking soda and baking powder into a bowl. Add enough water to make a hard dough.

2. Break the egg in a bowl, add sugar and milk. Whisk and incorporate the egg mixture gradually into the dough. Knead to make a soft but smooth dough, cover with a moist cloth and keep aside for 10 minutes.

3. Add oil, knead and punch the dough, cover with a moist cloth and keep aside for another 2 hours to allow the dough to rise.

4. Heat the oven till moderately hot—175 °C (350 °F).

5. Divide the dough into 6 portions. Make balls and place on a lightly floured surface. Sprinkle onion and melon seeds, flatten the balls slightly, cover and keep aside for 5 minutes.

6. Flatten each ball between the palms to make a round disc 0.25 cm thick and 5 cms in diameter, and then stretch on one side to make the shape of an elongated oval.

7. Place the naan on a greased baking tray and bake for 2-3 minutes.

To Serve:

Serve immediately.

Peshawari Naan

Fluffy leavened bread

Serves: 4-5   Preparation time: 45 minutes   Cooking time: 8-10 minutes

Ingredients:

Plain flour	500 gms/2½ cups	Onion seeds (kalonji)	5 gms/1 tsp
Baking powder	5 gms/1 tsp	Salt to taste	
Eggs, whisked	2	Sugar	12 gms/2½ tsp
Fennel seeds (saunf), ground	5 gms/1 tsp	Water	250 ml/1¼ cups
Ghee (clarified butter)	50 ml/¼ cup		

Method:

Step 1. Sieve together the flour and the baking powder in a mixing bowl.
2. Make a well in the centre and add the salt, sugar, three-fourths of the whisked egg mixture, ghee and fennel powder. Knead with water to make a medium soft dough. Cover with a moist cloth and keep aside for 30 minutes.
3. Divide into 10 equal portions and flatten each into a disc of 10 cm or 4" in diameter. Roll out each disk to a 12.75 cm or 5" round on floured board.
4. Preheat the oven to 175 °C (350 °F). Brush the naan with the remaining beaten eggs and sprinkle with onion seeds. Bake for 8-10 minutes, or until the bottom of the naan is golden and crisp.

To Serve:

A good accompaniment to all tandoori dishes.

Tandoori Roti

Oven-roasted bread

Serves: 4-5   Preparation time: 40 minutes   Cooking time: 5-8 minutes

Ingredients:

Whole wheat flour	500 gms/2½ cups	Salt to taste	
Butter to grease baking tray		Water	300 ml/1½ cups
Oil	15 ml/1 tbs		

Method:

Step 1. Flour and salt is sieved in a mixing bowl, the water mixed gradually, then the oil, and kneaded to a soft dough. Cover with a moist cloth and keep aside for half an hour.
2. Divide into 10 equal portions, make into balls, and dust with flour. Keep aside covered.
3. Flatten each ball between the palms to about 15 cm in diameter. Bake for 3 minutes in a greased baking tray, inside a preheated oven at 175 °C (350 °F).

To Serve:

Serve the rotis hot as soon as they are removed from the oven.

Khasta Roti

Whole wheat oven-baked bread

Serves: 4-5   Preparation time: 25 minutes   Cooking time: 10-15 minutes

Ingredients:

Whole wheat flour	500 gms/2½ cups	Sugar	12 gms/2½ tsp
Carom seeds (ajwain)	15 gms/3 tsp	Water	350 ml/1¾ cups
Salt to taste			

Method:

Step 1. To the sieved flour, add salt, sugar and ajwain. Knead to a hard dough with water. Cover with a moist cloth and keep aside for 15 minutes.
2. Divide the dough into 10 equal portions and roll into balls. Dust and roll into 10 cm rotis. Prick with a fork evenly.
3. Bake the rotis for 8-10 minutes in an oven at 175 °C (350 °F).

To Serve:

Serve with any vegetable purée.

Parantha

Whole wheat flakey pancake

Serves: 4-5   Preparation time: 20 minutes   Cooking time: 10 minutes

Ingredients:

Whole wheat flour	500 gms/2½ cups	Salt to taste	
Ghee for basting	200 gms/1 cup	Water	250 ml/1¼ cups
Oil	25ml/5 tsp		

Method:

Step 1. Sieve the flour and salt into a bowl. Add water gradually, and knead.

2. Incorporate 2 tbs of melted ghee and knead to a smooth dough.

3. Divide into 5 equal portions and make into balls. Dust with flour, cover and keep aside for 10 minutes.

4. Flatten the ball of dough and roll out. Apply a little ghee to the surface and fold over.
   Apply a little oil to the folded surface and fold over again. Roll out the triangle with a rolling pin.

5. Heat a *tawa*/griddle and apply a little ghee to the surface. Place the parantha on the tawa and
   cook for a few minutes. Coat with a little ghee and turn over and cook on the other side.

To Serve:

Remove and serve immediately.
NOTE: While making the dough, 4 tbs of chopped mint (pudina) or a mixture of chopped mint and
fenugreek (methi) may be added to the dough to make pudina paranthas or methi/pudina paranthas.

Bhatura

Deep-fried bread

Serves: 4-5   Preparation time: 1 hour   Cooking time: 20 minutes

Ingredients:

Plain flour	400 gms/2 cups	Salt to taste	
Baking powder	3 gms/²/₃ tsp	Semolina (sooji)	100 gms/½ cup
Baking soda	1.5 gms	Sugar	10 gms/2 tsp
Ghee (clarified butter)	20 gms/4 tsp	Water	150 ml/¾ cup
Oil for deep frying	500 ml/2½ cups	Yoghurt	25 gms/5 tsp

Method:

Step 1. Sieve the flour, semolina, baking powder, baking soda and salt into a bowl.

2. Whisk the yoghurt and the sugar together.

3. Mix the whisked yoghurt with the flour and add cold water, mixing to a dough.
   Cover the bowl and keep aside for 20 minutes.

4. Gradually add the ghee to the dough and mix. When fully mixed, knead to a fine, soft dough.
   Cover and set aside for 30 minutes.

5. Divide into 20 equal balls, cover and keep aside.

6. Roll out each ball of dough and pull it gently from both end to make an oval shape.
   Heat the oil in a *kadhai*/wok to smoking point. Deep fry each bhatura until it is golden on both sides.

To Serve:

Drain on a paper towel before serving.

Poori

Unleavened puffed pancake—a north Indian speciality

Serves: 4-5   Preparation time: **20** minutes   Cooking time: 10 minutes

Ingredients:

Whole wheat flour	250 gms/1¼ cups	Salt to taste	
Oil	10 ml/2 tsp	Water	125 ml/²⁄₃ cup
Refined oil for deep frying			

Method:

Step 1. Sieve the wheat flour and salt into a bowl. Add 10 ml of oil.
    2. Make a well in the sieved flour, add cold water to it and gradually start mixing to form a fine hard dough.
    3. Divide the dough into 25 equal size balls and place them on a lightly floured surface.
        Cover with a kitchen cloth for 5-10 minutes.
    4. Flatten each ball between the palms to make a circle, 4.5 cm in diameter.
        Roll out each of them to form a 10 cm disc.
    5. Heat the oil and deep fry the pooris until they puff up.

To Serve:

Drain on a paper towel before serving.

Bakarkhani

Bread with almonds and raisins

Serves: 4-5   Preparation time: 2 hours   Cooking time: 10 minutes

Ingredients:

Plain flour	500 gms/2½ cups	Green cardamom powder	2 gms/½ tsp
Almonds, blanched and slivered	15 gms/3 tsp	Milk, warmed	250 gms/1¼ cup
Baking powder	5 gms/1 tsp	Raisins	15 gms/3 tsp
Dry yeast	8 gms/1²⁄₃ tsp	Salt to taste	
Flour to dust		Sugar	15 gms/3 tsp
Ghee (clarified butter)	150 gms/¾ cup		

Method:

Step 1. Sieve the flour, baking powder and salt into a *paraat* (bowl).
    2. Dissolve the sugar in warm milk and stir.
    3. Dissolve the yeast in a little warm water and allow it to rise for 20 minutes.
    4. Soak almonds in water along with the raisins for half an hour and then drain.
    5. Make a well in the sieved flour and pour in the milk and dissolved yeast. Mix gradually to make a dough.
        When fully mixed, knead for a few minutes. Cover with a moist cloth and keep aside for 5 minutes.
    6. Add the melted ghee and incorporate gradually. When fully mixed, knead again to make a soft dough.
    7. Add the almonds, raisins and cardamom powder, knead, cover and keep in a warm place for
        half an hour to allow the dough to rise.
    8. Divide into 12 equal portions, make the dough balls, dust with flour, cover and keep aside for 10 minutes.
        Place the balls on a lightly floured surface and roll out into round discs, 8 cm in diameter.
        Prick the surfaces of the dough with a fork.
    9. Heat the oven to 175 °C (350 °F). Grease a baking tray with ghee, arrange the rolled out discs
        on it and bake for 8-10 minutes.

To Serve:

Brush the Bakarkhani with melted butter or ghee as soon as they are removed from the oven. Serve immediately.

Zafrani Biryani

A saffron-flavoured rice delicacy

Serves: 4-5   Preparation time: 50 minutes   Cooking time: 1 hour

Ingredients:

Chicken	1 kg	Green cardamoms	10
Rice, basmati or any long grain variety	500 gms/2½ cups	Green coriander	10 gms/2 tsp
Bay leaves (tej patta)	2	Lemon juice	10 ml/2 tsp
Black cardamoms	2	Mace (javitri)	5 gms/1 tsp
Black cumin seeds (shah jeera)	6 gms/1⅓ tsp	Milk	100 ml/½ cup
Butter, unsalted	150 gms/¾ cup	Mint leaves	10 gms/2 tsp
Cinnamon sticks	4	Onions, sliced	100 gms/½ cup
Cloves	10	Red chilli powder	10 gms/2 tsp
Cream	50 ml/¼ cup	Saffron	0.5 gms
Garlic paste	40 gms/2⅔ tbs	Salt to taste	
Ginger paste	40 gms/2⅔ tbs	Water	4-4.2 litres
		Yoghurt	600 gms/3 cups

Method:

Step 1. Clean, skin and cut the chicken into 8 pieces.

2. Wash the rice and soak it for at least half an hour.

3. Whisk the yoghurt in a bowl and divide into two equal portions. Dissolve the saffron in warm milk and cream. Add one portion of the yoghurt to it. Add the mint and green coriander to this.

4. Preheat the oven to 150 ºC (300 ºF).

5. In a large saucepan boil 4 litres of water and add one bay leaf, 2 green cardamoms and 2 cloves. Add the washed rice and salt to taste, and boil for a few minutes until the rice is half cooked. Drain the rice with the whole spices and keep hot.

6. Heat butter in a large saucepan, add the remaining whole spices and black cumin and sauté over medium heat until the cumin seeds begin to crackle. Add the onions and sauté until golden brown. Add the ginger and garlic pastes and red chillies and stir for 15 seconds.

7. Add the chicken and salt to taste and cook for a further 3-4 minutes.

8. Add the second portion of plain yoghurt along with approximately 200 ml of water, stir and bring to a boil. Lower the heat and simmer until the chicken is almost done. Stir in lemon juice and check the seasoning.

9. To assemble the biryani, grease the base of a large baking dish. Spread half the chicken mixture, sprinkle half of the saffron/yoghurt/mint/coriander mixture over this. Now spread half the parboiled rice over this. Cover this once again with the remaining chicken, then with the remaining rice and sprinkle the remaining yoghurt mixture over the rice. Place a moist cloth over this, put a lid on the dish and seal it with dough.
10. Bake in the oven for 10-15 minutes on *dum* or preheated oven at 150 ºC (300 ºF).

To Serve:

Remove from oven, serve hot garnished with golden fried almonds.

Parda Chilman Biryani

A mutton biryani with a layer of pastry on the top to seal in the fragrance

Serves: 4-5   Preparation time: 50 minutes   Cooking time: 1 hour

Ingredients:

Lamb chops on a single bone	1 kg	Lemon juice	5 gms/1 tsp
Rice, basmati or any long grain variety	600 gms/3 cups	Mace powder (javitri)	3 gms/²/₃ tsp
Bay leaves (tej patta)	2	Milk	30 ml/2 tbs
Black cumin seeds (shah jeera)	6 gms/1¹/₃ tsp	Mint leaves	10 gms/2 tsp
Butter, unsalted	200 gms/1 cup	Oil	50 ml/¼ cup
Cinnamon sticks	2	Onion paste	100 gms/½ cup
Cloves	10	Onions, sliced and fried	50 gms/¼ cup
Cream	50 ml/¼ cup	Red chillies	6
Eggs, beaten	2	Saffron	0.5 gms
Flour	600 gms/3 cups	Salt to taste	
Garlic paste	45 gms/3 tbs	Vetivier (kewda)	3 drops
Ginger paste	45 gms/3 tbs	Water or lamb stock	200 ml/1 cup
Green cardamoms	10	Yellow chilli powder (deghi mirch)	10 gms/2 tsp
Green coriander	10 gms/2 tsp	Yoghurt	300 gms/1½ cups

Method:

Step 1. Wash the rice and soak it for at least 30 minutes.
2. Whisk the yoghurt in a bowl and divide into two equal portions. Dissolve the saffron in warm milk and cream. Add vetivier drops and one portion of yoghurt. Add one portion of the yoghurt to it. Add the mint and green coriander to this.
3. Preheat the oven to 150 ºC (300 ºF).
4. In a large saucepan boil 4 litres of water and add one bay leaf, 1 cinnamon stick, 2 green cardamoms, 2 cloves and salt to taste. Add the washed rice and boil for a few minutes until it is half done. Drain the rice with the whole spices and keep hot.
5. Heat the oil in a large saucepan and add the remaining whole spices and black cumin and sauté over medium heat until the cumin seeds begin to crackle. Add the onion paste and sauté until golden brown. Add the ginger and garlic pastes, red chillies and yellow chilli powder and stir for 15 seconds.
6. Add the lamb chops and salt and cook for a further 3-4 minutes. Add a portion of the plain yoghurt and approximately 200 ml of water, stir and bring to a boil. Lower the heat and simmer until the chops are almost done. Check the seasoning.
7. To assemble the biryani, grease the base of a large baking dish. Spread half the chops mixture, sprinkle half of the saffron/yoghurt/mint/coriander mixture over this. Now spread half the parboiled rice over this. Cover this once again with the remaining chops, cover with the remaining rice and sprinkle the remaining yoghurt mixture over the rice. Also sprinkle mace powder, fried sliced onions and lemon juice.
8. Crumble the butter into the flour, add one egg and enough milk to make a stiff dough. Roll out the dough and cover the rice and lamb mixture with it. Seal the edges and brush with the other beaten egg.
9. Bake in the oven for 10-15 minutes on *dum*.

To Serve:

Break the pastry seal and serve hot with garlic raita.

Anokhi Biryani

A delightful blend of rice and pulses

Serves: 4-5   Preparation time: 2 hours   Cooking time: 45 minutes

Ingredients:

Chana dal (split bengal gram)	25 gms/5 tsp	Mint leaves, chopped	10 gms/2 tsp
Kidney beans (rajma)	25 gms/5 tsp	Onion rings, fried	20 gms/¼ cup
Mung dal (split green beans), washed	25 gms/5 tsp	Refined oil	50 ml/3⅓ tbs
Rice	150 gms/¾ cup	Salt to taste	
Toovar dal (pigeon peas)	25 gms/5 tsp	Tomatoes, skinned and deseeded	120 gms/⅔ cup
Almonds, blanched and fried	50 gms/¼ cup	Water	500 ml/2½ cups
Bay leaves (tej patta)	2		
Butter	30 gms/2 tbs	**Spices to be ground:**	
Cinnamon sticks	3	Coriander powder	10 gms/2 tsp
Cloves	6	Cumin powder (jeera)	5 gms/1 tsp
Garlic, chopped	6 gms/1⅓ tsp	Fresh coconut, grated	150 gms/¾ cup
Green cardamoms	15	Red chilli powder	5 gms/1 tsp
Green chillies, slit and deseeded	10 gms		

Method:

Step 1. In a food processor grind the coconut, red chilli powder, coriander powder and cumin powder with a quarter cup of water to a fine paste.
2. Clean, wash and soak together the rajma, toovar dal, chana dal for 1 hour.
3. Clean, wash and soak the rice and the mung dal in a separate container for 1 hour.
4. Strain the three pulses. Add 150 ml/¾ cup of water and cook over medium heat until tender.
5. Strain the rice, mung dal mixture. Add 1½ cups of water and cook over medium heat until almost cooked. Drain excess water and keep the water aside.
6. Heat the oil in a pan. Add cinnamon sticks, cloves and bay leaves, green cardamoms and sauté for 30 seconds. Add the chopped garlic, tomatoes and paste mixture prepared in Step 1 and cook for 4-5 minutes or till the oil separates.
7. Add all the pulses and rice to the pan. Sprinkle a quarter cup of reserved rice. Add salt. Cover and cook on low heat until rice is fully cooked.

To Serve:

Remove from heat and garnish with fried onion rings, fried almonds, mint leaves and green chillies and dot with butter.

Vegetable Pulao

Combination of long grain rice and vegetables of the season cooked with exotic condiments

Serves: 4-5   Preparation time: 45 minutes   Cooking time: 30 minutes

Ingredients:

Rice, basmati or any long grain variety	200 gms/1 cup	Onions, chopped	50 gms/¼ cup
Carrots, diced and parboiled	20 gms/4 tsp	Red chilli powder	3 gms/⅔ tsp
Cauliflower, small pieces	20 gms/4 tsp	Refined oil	60 ml/4 tbs
Green peas, parboiled	20 gms/4 tsp	Salt to taste	
Mushrooms quartered	20 gms/4 tsp	Water	500 ml/2½ cups
Bay leaf (tej patta)	1	White pepper powder	2 gms/½ tsp
Black cumin (shah jeera)	5 gms/1 tsp		
Cinnamon stick, medium	1	**For garnishing:**	
Cloves	4	Cashewnuts, fried golden	10
Ginger paste	10 gms/2 tsp	Coriander, chopped	5 gms/1 tsp
Green cardamom	3	Cream	30 ml/2 tbs

Ginger juliennes	3 gms/²/₃ tsp	Mace powder (javitri)	2 gms/½ tsp
Green chillies, slit	5 gms/1 tsp	Onions, fried	10 gms/1 onion
Lemon juice	15 ml/1 tbs		

Method:

Step 1. Clean, wash and soak the rice in water for 30 minutes.

2. Heat the oil in a heavy saucepan, add the cloves, cinnamon stick, bay leaf, cardamom and black cumin seeds and sauté over medium heat until they begin to crackle.

3. Add the chopped onions, stir and cook till soft. Add the ginger paste and red chilli powder, stir and then add all the vegetables alongwith white pepper and salt. Cook for 3-4 minutes.

4. Add the washed and drained rice, stir carefully, add water to the rice and bring it to a quick boil. Lower the heat, cover and cook till the rice is almost done.

5. Remove the lid and sprinkle with the ginger juliennes, slit green chillies, fried onions, mace powder, lemon juice, cashewnut, green coriander and cream.

6. Seal lid with dough, cook on very low heat for 10-15 minutes, or in a very slow oven for 10 minutes.

To Serve:

Serve hot with mint raita.
NOTE: To prepare **Zafrani Pulao**, do not use any of the vegetables. Follow the same method as given above.

Noormehal Pulao

A combination of small and large pearls

Serves: 4-5   Preparation time: 45 minutes   Cooking time: 45 minutes

Ingredients:

Rice, basmati or any long grain variety	400 gms/2 cups	Green cardamoms	8
Bay leaf (tej patta)	1	Green coriander, chopped	10 gms/1 tsp
Black cumin seed (shah jeera)	3 gms/²/₃ tsp	Mace powder (javitri)	3 gms/²/₃ tsp
Black peppercorns	10	Onions, finely chopped	50 gms/¼ cup
Butter	30 gms/2 tbs	Cottage cheese (paneer)	100 gms/½ cup
Cinnamon stick, medium	3	Refined oil	60 ml/4 tbs
Cloves	6	Saffron strands	1 gm
Cream/milk	50 ml/3¹/₃ tbs	Salt to taste	
Garam masala	10 gms/2 tsp	Spinach (palak) juice, optional	10 ml/2 tsp
Ginger paste	12 gms/2½ tsp	Water/stock	500 ml/2½ cups

Method:

Step 1. Clean, wash and soak the rice in water for 30 minutes.

2. Heat the oil in a heavy pot, add the bay leaf, cinnamon stick, cloves, black cumin seed, cardamom and peppercorns and sauté over medium heat till the spices begin to crackle.

3. Add onions, stir and cook till soft and golden. Add ginger paste and garam masala and sauté for 30-40 seconds.

4. Add the washed, drained rice, stir and cook over medium heat for 3-4 minutes. Add water or chicken stock to the rice. Bring rice to a quick boil, add salt to taste, lower the heat, cover and cook till the rice is done and the liquid evaporated.

5. While rice is cooking, grate the paneer very finely in a bowl. Using a wooden spoon moisten paneer with 10 ml of cream/milk. Season with salt. Divide this mixture into three portions. Mix one portion with the saffron which is dissolved in 10 ml of cream/milk, the second portion with spinach juice and leave the third portion as it is.

6. Make small balls of 4-5 gms each from these three mixtures. Carefully fry them in butter. These balls are called the Noormehal.

7. To the remaining cream/milk add the mace powder and keep aside.

To Serve:

Transfer the pulao to a serving platter. Garnish with three different paneer balls, green coriander and lace with cream/milk mixture. Serve with pineapple raita.

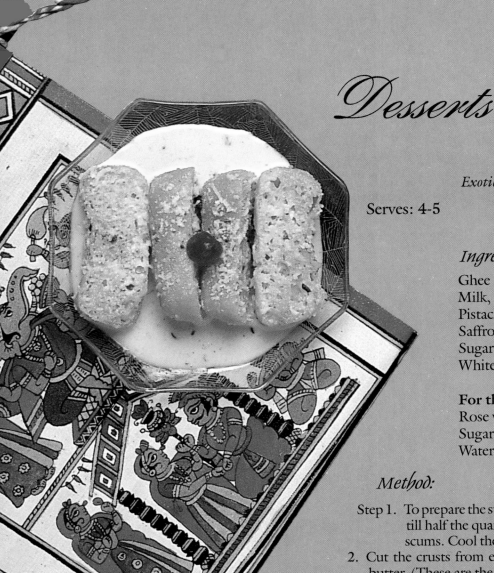

Desserts

Shahi Tukda

Exotic dessert from the court of nawabs

Serves: 4-5   Preparation time: 10 minutes
Cooking time: 50 minutes

Ingredients:

Ghee (clarified butter)	150 gms/¾ cup
Milk, full cream	1 litre/5 cups
Pistachios	25 gms/5 tsp
Saffron (dissolved in 1 tbs warm milk)	1 gm/¼ tsp
Sugar	300 gms/1½ cups
White bread (cut into ¾" slices)	10 slices

For the sugar syrup:

Rose water (gulab jal)	4 drops
Sugar	60 gms/4 tbs
Water	200 ml/1 cup

Method:

Step 1. To prepare the sugar syrup, put water and sugar together to boil. Boil till half the quantity of liquid is left. From time to time remove the scums. Cool the syrup and add the rose water.

2. Cut the crusts from each bread slice. Fry to a golden colour in clarified butter. (These are the tukdas.)

3. Soak these tukdas in the cooled syrup.

4. Take a heavy bottomed pot and bring the milk to a boil on a medium heat. Simmer milk for 30-45 minutes (uncovered), until its consistency is slightly thick, and its colour a pale yellow.

5. Gradually stir in the sugar.

6. Cook for another 3-4 minutes, until the sugar is completely dissolved. (This milk concentrate is called rabri.)

7. Cool and chill.

To Serve:

Arrange each fried tukda on a platter. Pour the chilled rabri over the fried tukdas. Garnish with chopped pistachios and laced with saffron cream.

NOTE: Hot rabri may also be used to top the tukda instead of chilled rabri.

Pista Rasmalai

Cream cheese covered with thickened milk

Serves: 4-5   Preparation time: 45 minutes   Cooking time: 45 minutes

Ingredients:

For the chenna:

Lemon juice	15 ml/1 tbs
Milk	2 litres/10 cups

For the chenna balls:

Baking powder	3-4 gms/⅔-¾ tsp
Flour	20 gms/4 tsp
Sugar	900 gms/4½ cups

Water	4 cups

For the rabri:

Milk, full cream	500 ml/2½ cups
Pistachios (blanched, skinned and chopped)	25 gms/5 tsp
Sugar	100 gms/½ cup

Method:

To make the chenna:

Step 1. In a pan heat the milk and bring it to a slow boil. Remove from the heat and let it cool for 3-4 minutes.
    2. Add lemon juice and stir and wait until the milk curdles.
    3. Carefully strain the curdled milk through a fine cheese cloth. Tie it up and let it hang for 30 minutes or until the liquid has completely drained off. The residue in the cheese cloth is called chenna or cream cheese.
    4. Place the chenna in a bowl. Gradually break it up with your fingers and rub with your palm to a creamy texture.
    5. Sieve flour and baking powder together, add the chenna and knead to a fine soft dough.
    6. Divide the dough into 20 equal parts. Roll each portion into a ball. Flatten the balls slightly between your palms.
    7. In a heavy pan bring 4 cups of water to a slow boil. Add 900 gms of sugar and dissolve it over low heat to get a fine, clear syrup. Remove the scum from the surface. Add the chenna balls to the syrup and keep syrup on the boil on low heat till the balls double in size and rise to the surface (10 minutes).
    8. Remove each ball with a slotted spoon, and keep it aside for 3-4 minutes. Drain any syrup and place on the serving dish.

To make the rich creamy milk coating (rabri):

    9. While the chenna balls are being cooked in the sugar syrup, reduce the milk for the rabri to half on low heat, stirring occasionally. Add the sugar, cool and refrigerate.

To Serve:

Pour the chilled rich milk sauce over the chenna balls and let them stand in the refrigerator for at least 30 minutes. Sprinkle with chopped pistachio nuts (or saffron dissolved in a little rabri).

NOTE: Add saffron and 4-5 drops of rose water to the **Pista Rasmalai** and turn it into **Kesari Rasmalai** (saffron cream).

Gulab Jamun

A sweet made from cottage cheese

Serves: 4-5	Preparation time: 20 minutes	Cooking time: 2½ hours

Ingredients:

Cottage cheese (paneer)	70 gms/4⅓ tbs	Pistachios, blanched, skinned	
Baking soda	3 gms/⅔ tsp	and chopped	25 gms/5 tsp
Cardamom powder	2 gms/½ tsp	Saffron, dissolved in 15 ml of milk	1 gm/¼ tsp
Flour	60 gms/4 tbs	Sugar	1 kg/5 cups
Khoya (dried milk)	500 gms/2½ cups	Water	500 ml/2½ cups
Oil (for frying)	500 ml/ 2½ cups		

Method:

Step 1. In a bowl break up the khoya, mix the paneer and rub the mixture to a fine creamy texture.
    2. Sieve the flour and baking soda together, mix with the khoya mixture and knead to a soft dough.
    3. Divide the dough into 20 equal-size balls and cover with a moist cloth.
    4. In a pan boil together the water and sugar, removing the scum from time to time. Cook on low heat until the syrup has a one-thread consistency.
    5. In a bowl combine the chopped pistachios, saffron dissolved in milk and cardamom powder into a thick paste. Divide the paste into 20 small balls.
    6. Insert each ball into one of the paneer dumplings and seal and make balls.
    7. Heat the oil in a pan. Fry the dumplings over very slow heat, till they are golden in colour. Remove them from the oil with a slotted spoon and immediately transfer into the sugar syrup. Leave in the syrup for at least 1-2 hours.

To Serve:

Serve hot with the syrup.

Badami Kheer

A creamy, aromatic rice and almond cream

Serves: 4-5   Preparation time: 30 minutes   Cooking time: 30 minutes

Ingredients:

Almonds, blanched and halved	50 gms/¼ cup	Red cherries (for the garnish)	20 gms/4 tsp
Green cardamom	6 gms/1⅓ tsp	Rose water (gulab jal)	4-5 drops
Lemon rind, grated	1 tsp	Salt to taste	
Long-grain rice	100 gms/½ cup	Sugar	150 gms/¾ cup
Milk, full cream	1 litre/5 cups		

Method:

Step 1. Soak the rice in water for 30 minutes.
2. In a heavy pan heat the milk and bring to a slow boil over medium heat. Add the drained rice, green cardamoms and lemon rind and continue to cook over medium heat until the rice is slightly over cooked.
3. Add the sugar and almonds and cook for 5-10 minutes stirring from time to time with a wooden spoon. Check the consistency—it should be quite thick and have a slightly golden colour.

To Serve:

Add salt, rose water and cherries. Serve hot or cold.

Gajrela

A north Indian dessert made mainly in winter when carrots are in season

Serves: 4-5   Preparation time: 10 minutes   Cooking time: 1 hour

Ingredients:

Carrots, finely grated	1 kg	Milk, full cream	1 litre/5 cups
Almonds	100 gms/½ cup	Pistachios	50 gms/¼ cup
Ghee (clarified butter)	60 ml/4 tbs	Sugar	180 gms/1 scant cup
Green cardamoms	10		

Method:

Step 1. In a heavy pan bring the milk to a slow boil, stirring with a wooden spoon.
2. Add the grated carrots and green cardamoms and cook over medium heat for 30-45 minutes or until the milk is almost evaporated.
3. Add the sugar, stir and cook until the sugar is completely dissolved.
4. Add the ghee, stir and cook until the carrots are slightly caramelized.
5. Reduce the heat, add the almonds and pistachios, and cook for 3-4 minutes.

To Serve:

Serve hot. Garnish with pistachio/almond flakes and grated khoya.

Phirni

A dessert that originated in the Arab countries

Serves: 4-5   Preparation time: 10 minutes   Cooking time: 30 minutes

Ingredients:

Cardamom powder	3 gms/⅔ tsp	Rice flour	100 gms/½ cup
or rose water	4-5 drops	Saffron dissolved in 15 ml milk	1 gm/¼ tsp
Milk, full cream	1 litre/5 cups	Salt	a pinch
Pistachios	50 gms/¼ cup	Sugar	200 gms/1 cup

Method:

Step 1. In a heavy pan, heat half the milk and bring to a slow boil.
2. Dissolve the rice flour in the remaining cold milk and slowly add to the hot milk. Continue to cook over very low heat, stirring constantly until the mixture becomes a thick, light custard.
3. Add sugar and the pinch of salt and cook for 2-3 minutes until the sugar is completely dissolved.
4. Cool, add the rose water and mix well.

To Serve:

Serve individually in bowls or in a large bowl, garnished with chopped pistachios and saffron cream.

Badam ka Halwa

A rich almond dessert

Serves: 4-5   Preparation time: 30 minutes   Cooking time: 20 minutes

Ingredients:

Almonds, blanched and chopped	500 gms/2½ cups	Saffron	1 gm/¼ tsp
Cardamom powder	6 gms/1⅓ tsp	Silver leaves (varq)	optional
Ghee (clarified butter)	200 gms/1 cup	Sugar	500 gms/2½ cups
Milk	200 gms/1 cup		

Method:

Step 1. In a food processor grind the almonds with a little milk to a fine paste.

2. Heat ghee in a heavy pan. Add the almond paste and cook over medium heat until the almond paste becomes light golden. Add the milk and sugar and cook over medium heat for 10-15 minutes, until the moisture evaporates and the mixture becomes thick. Remove from heat.

3. Add cardamom powder and saffron.

To Serve:

To serve cold: spread on a greased flat tray, cut into small square pieces and decorate with silver leaves.

To serve hot: ladle individual portion on a dessert plate and decorate with silver leaves.

Pista Kulfi

Icecream flavoured with pistachios

Serves: 4-5   Preparation time: 10 minutes   Cooking time: 3 hours

Ingredients:

Cardamom powder	3 gms/⅔ tsp	Pistachios, chopped	100 gm/½ cup
Cherries, chopped	10	Sugar	400 gms/2 cups
Milk, full cream	4 litres/20 cups		

Method:

Step 1. In a pan bring milk to a boil over medium heat and continue to boil over a medium heat till the quantity has halved (30-45 minutes). The consistency should be slightly thick and the colour, pale yellow.

2. Gradually add the sugar, stir and cook for another 3-4 minutes until the sugar is completely dissolved.

3. Cool and add chopped pistachios, cardamom powder and cherries.

4. Fill in small aluminum conical-shaped containers or small even-sized containers. Seal the tops with silver foil and freeze for 1½-2 hours.

To Serve:

Demould and serve chilled with faluda (cold vermicelli).

Rabri

Thick sweetened milk

Serves: 4-5   Preparation time: 10 minutes   Cooking time: 1 hour

Ingredients:

Milk, full cream	2 litre/8 cups	Sugar	200 gms/2 cups
Almonds, blanched, skinned and chopped	25 gms/5 tsp	Saffron, dissolved in 10 ml milk (optional)	1 gm/¼ tsp
Pistachios, blanched, skinned and halved	50 gms/3⅓ tbs	or rose water (gulab jal)	3 drops

Method:

Step 1. In a pan bring milk to a boil over medium heat and continue boiling for about 30-45 minutes till the quantity has halved. The consistency should be slightly thick and the colour, pale yellow.

2. Gradually add the sugar, stir and cook for another 15-20 minutes until the sugar is completely dissolved.

To Serve:

Transfer to a serving bowl. Cool and add the pistachios, almonds and dissolved saffron mixture or rose water. Garnish with silver leaves or gold leaves (optional). Serve chilled.

Glossary

Alu: Potato.

Amchoor: Dried mango powder. Amchoor gives food a slight sourness. Lemon juice may be used as a substitute.

Aniseed (Sweet cumin): Aromatic seeds used in meat dishes. Also eaten as a digestive after meals.

Aromatic garam masala (Chana masala): Ingredients: Green cardamoms 175 gms; cumin seeds 120 gms; black pepper corns 120 gms; cinnamon (2.5 cms) 25 sticks; cloves 15 gms; nutmeg, 2. Makes 440 gms. Method: Grind all the ingredients in a food processor to make a fine powder. Sieve and store in a sterilized container.

Atta (Whole wheat flour): A finely ground whole wheat flour used for making Indian breads. Use a combination of whole wheat and plain flour if atta is not available.

Asafoetida (Heeng): A pungent grainy powder used mainly for its digestive properties.

Baigan (Aubergine, Egg plant, Brinjal): Used whole, or in pieces. May be broiled (whole) to make pulp for curry.

Basmati rice: A fine long-grain rice. Any long-grain rice may be used as a substitute.

Bay leaf (Tej patta): An aromatic herb used for flavouring vegetable and meat dishes.

Black beans (Urad dal): May be used whole or split; is boiled and puréed to make dal.

Black lentils (Masoor dal): Also known as red split lentils.

Capsicum: Green pepper.

Cardamom, green (Chhoti elaichi): An aromatic spice, generally sold in its pod; used whole in pods or with its seeds ground.

Cardamom, large black (Badi elaichi): A spice used in many vegetable and meat dishes. The black pods are ground whole.

Carom seeds (Ajwain): Also known as thymol or omum seeds; used in pickles and vegetable dishes.

Cauliflower (Gobi): Used whole or as flowerets to make a dry curry.

Chaat masala: Ingredients: Cumin seeds 65 gms; black pepper corns 60 gms; black salt (pound before putting in the grinder) 60 gms; dry mint leaves 30 gms; carom seeds 5 gms; asafoetida (pound before putting in the grinder) 5 gms; mango powder 150 gms; salt 60 gms; ginger powder 20 gms; yellow chilli powder 20 gms. Makes 445 gms. Method: Grind cumin seeds, pepper corns, mint leaves and asafoetida together in a food processor. Transfer to a clean and dry bowl and mix all the remaining ingredients. Sieve and store in a dry, airtight container.

Chillies, green (Hari mirch): Fresh chillies used for flavouring, tempering curries and dals. Sometimes chopped, sometimes ground into a paste.

Chillies, whole dried red (Sabut lal mirch): Hotter than green chillies; used like them.

Chilli powder (Pisi hui lal mirch): Ground dried red chillies. The nearest equivalent is red cayenne pepper powder.

Cinnamon (Dalchini): Available in powder or stick form; used in curries and pulaos.

Cloves (Lavang): Dried flower buds, available whole; used in savouries and for pickling.

Coconut, grated fresh: Method: Crack open the coconut into two halves. Remove the coconut flesh from the hard shell with a knife, break the flesh into 2.5 cm or 1" pieces and finely grate the pieces using a hand grater or grind in a food processor. Grated coconut freezes well and defrosts quickly.

Coconut milk, fresh: Method: Put 2 cups of grated coconut into a food processor. Add 1¼ cups of very hot water. Blend for a few seconds. Put the contents of the blender into a sieve and squeeze out all the liquid.

Coconut milk, tinned: Excellent quality tinned coconut milk is available.

Coconut, creamed: Creamed coconut is easily available and can be converted into coconut milk by adding water (²/₃ cup of hot water to ¹/₃ cup of creamed coconut).

Coriander, fresh green/Chinese parsley (Hara dhania): The leaves are used for seasoning and for garnishing.

Coriander seeds, whole/ground (Dhania): Seeds of the coriander plant. Available as whole seeds or in powdered form.

Cottage cheese (Paneer): Method: Boil 3 litres of milk. Add the juice of one lemon and stir till the mixture curdles. Remove from the fire. Cover and keep aside for 10 minutes. Strain the mixture through a piece of cheese cloth. Tie the ends of cloth together and squeeze out all the liquid. The solid portion left in the cheese cloth should now be placed under a heavy weight for a few hours. The block of cottage cheese (300 gms) is now ready for use. Tofu can be used as a substitute.

Cumin seeds, whole/ground (Jeera): Available as whole seeds; may be powdered.

Cumin seeds, black (Shah jeera, Kala jeera): A caraway-like seed with a flavour that is more subtle than that of ordinary cumin; to be used in small quantities.

Curry leaves, fresh and dried (Kari patta): Highly aromatic leaves, shaped like small bay leaves. Use fresh leaves or the less aromatic dried ones.

Dals: Dried, split lentils, although the word is used loosely for all pulses (legumes), dried beans and split peas.

Dried milk (Khoya): A milk preparation made from milk powder and water or from boiling creamy milk; used in sweet dishes and Mughlai cooking. Can be bought in blocks.

Dum cooking: Cooking by steam. This technique is used when a dish is almost cooked and needs slow cooking to improve its flavour. The pan is generally covered and sealed with dough and cooked on a low flame. The nearest equivalent is very gentle casseroling in the oven with the dish covered.

Dum ka masala: Ingredients: Fennel seeds 45 gms; ginger powder 45 gms; black cardamoms 20 gms; green cardamoms 20 gms. Makes 125 gms. Method: Grind all the ingredients in a food processor to a fine powder. Sieve and store in a sterilized airtight container. *Note*: A pinch of this masala is added to the dish before the handi is sealed and put on *dum*. It adds to the aroma.

Fennel seeds (Saunf): These seeds are larger but look and taste like aniseeds.

Fenugreek leaves (Methi): A popular leafy vegetable, considered to be a great delicacy.

Fenugreek seeds (Methi): Yellow, square and flat, the seeds have a slightly bitter flavour.

Gajjar (Carrot): Can be made into a dry curry or halwa.

Garam masala: An exotic mixture of herbs and spices. Ingredients: Cumin seeds 90 gms; black pepper corns 70 gms; black cardamom seeds 75 gms; fennel seeds 30 gms; green cardamoms 40 gms; coriander seeds 30 gms; cloves 20 gms; cinnamon (2.5 cms) 20 sticks; mace powder 20 gms; black cumin seeds 20 gms; dry rose petals 15 gms; bay leaves 15 gms; ginger powder 15 gms; nutmeg 3. Makes 445 gms. Method: Put all the ingredients, except the ginger powder, in a food processor and grind to a fine powder. Transfer the masala to a clean and dry bowl, add ginger powder and mix well. Sieve and store in a sterilized, dry, airtight container.

Ghee (Clarified butter): Ready-made ghee is easily available.

Ginger (Adrak): Ginger root has a pungent flavour. Its potato-like skin is to be peeled before it can be chopped or grated.

Gram flour (Besan): A binding agent, used mainly as a batter.

Kadhai: The Indian wok, made out of iron or aluminium or stainless steel. It is excellent for stir frying and its rounded bottom makes it very economical for deep frying.

Kasoori methi (Fenugreek leaves, dried): A rare herb grown in the Kasoor region of Pakistan. The dried leaves, readily available in handy packets, are largely used in chicken and lamb preparations to give the dishes a sweet aroma.

Kewda (Vetivier): An extract made from the flowers of the kewda plant (pandanus). Adds fragrance. Kewda essence is available in bottles.

Lagan cooking: Lagan cooking is done directly on a thick bottomed griddle on a low flame.

Mace (Javitri): The outer membrane of nutmeg, with a similar taste; available as blades or powder. Used in meat dishes.

Maize flour (Makke ka atta): Flour made from Indian corn.

Melon seeds (Magaz): Peeled melon seeds are used in savoury dishes.

Mint leaves (Pudina): A fresh herb, used in raitas and chutneys and for garnishing yoghurt-based dishes.

Moong dal (Split green lentils): This dal (or lentil) is sold both hulled and unhulled.

Mustard oil (Sarson ka tel): A yellow oil, extracted from mustard seeds, pungent while raw, and sweet when heated.

Mustard seeds, whole black (Sarson): Tiny, dark, round seeds, black or reddish-brown. Used for tempering in dals and pickles.

Nigella seeds (Kalonji): Sprinkled over Indian oven breads and used in cooking vegetables and fish.

Nutmeg (Jaiphal): Used grated or ground, for flavouring sweets and savouries.

Paraat: Wide, flat-bottomed mixing bowl used for kneading dough. Any mixing bowl may be substituted.

Parsley: A stand-in herb for green coriander leaves. Used for garnishing and flavouring savoury dishes.

Pistachios (Pista): Used in sweetmeats and biryanis.

Pomegranate seeds (Anardana): Seeds used in making savouries, and for giving a sour flavour.

Poppy seeds (Khus khus): Tiny white seeds.

Pressure cooking: A great time saver. Pressure cooking is not suitable for cooking vegetables the Indian way, but it is ideal for cooking meat and lentils. All cooking is done at 15 lb pressure and compared to the traditional method only half the liquid and only 15 minutes are needed to cook.. Do check manufacturing instructions for exact time applicable to quantities being cooked.

Rose water (Gulab jal): A liquid extract of fresh rose petals. Used for flavouring sweet dishes.

Saffron (Kesar/Zafran): The stigma of the crocus flower, grown in the Kashmir valley. Known as the king of spices, it is used for its rich yellow colouring and for its flavour. Dissolve in water or warm milk to use as saffron cream.

Sambar powder: Ingredients: Coriander seeds 150 gms; cumin seeds 100 gms; black pepper corns 40 gms; mustard seeds 40 gms; fenugreek seeds 40 gms; red chilli, whole 40 gms; turmeric powder 25 gms; Bengal gram 80 gms; urad dal 80 gms; oil 50 ml; garlic powder 20 gms; ginger powder 20 gms; Makes 600 gms. Method: In a pan, heat the oil and sauté all the ingredients on very low heat until they are evenly coloured and they release an aroma. Cool and grind to a fine powder.

Sesame seeds (Til): Beige coloured seeds used in making bread.

Split green beans (Moong beans, dried or Moong ki dal): Used for making purées and other dal preparations.

Spinach: Palak

Tamarind (Imli): A pod-like, sour fruit, used for making sauces and chutneys. Tamarind pulp and bottled concentrate is readily available.

Tandoor/Tandoori cooking: Tandoori food gets its name from the *tandoor* or the clay oven in which it is baked. This cooking originated in the North West Frontier Provinces, now in Pakistan.

Tandoori chaat masala: Ingredients: Cumin seeds 50 gms; black pepper corns 50 gms; black salt (pound before putting in the grinder) 50 gms; dry mint leaves 25 gms; fenugreek 20 gms; green cardamoms 30 gms; cloves 15 gms; cinnamon sticks 5; ajwain 5 gms; mace 2 gms; amchoor 125 gms; salt to taste; ginger powder 20 gms; yellow chill powder 20 gms. Makes 425 gms. Method: Put all the ingredients, except the amchoor, salt, ginger powder and yellow chilli powder in a food processor and grind to a fine powder. Transfer to a clean, dry bowl. Add the remaining ingredients and mix well. Sieve and store in a sterilized, dry, airtight container.

Tava: A slightly curved, cast-iron griddle used for making Indian breads.

Turmeric (Haldi): Yellow, powdered spice, used for colouring and flavouring.

Toovar dal (Pigeon peas): Also known as toor dal and arhar dal.

Yoghurt (Dahi): Made from milk and used extensively in making curries and biryani.

95

Index to Recipes

NOTE: Abreviations used within parenthesis: C = Chicken preparations; D = Desserts; F = Fish and Seafood; L = Lamb preparations, R = Rotis and Rice; V = Vegetables and Paneer preparations.